In this compact but powerful analysis of American life and thought in the years since the Second World War, George Marsden shows why neither a triumphant secular liberalism nor a restored religious consensus can serve as a rallying point for national unity. Instead, he makes a case for a pluralism that treats the widest possible range of religious and nonreligious perspectives as equally deserving of protections and recognition, and rejects the privatization of religious speech and expression. The result is a book that is as much about dawning as about twilight, one that not only provides a fresh and compelling view of postwar America, but offers a fresh vision of the road ahead, a future in which our emerging debates over the meaning and limits of religious liberty will be of central and growing importance.

—Wilfred M. McClay, G.T. and Libby Blankenship Chair in the History of Liberty, University of Oklahoma

THE TWILIGHT
OF THE AMERICAN
ENLIGHTENMENT

THE TWILIGHT
OF THE AMERICAN
ENLIGHTENMENT

The 1950s *and the* CRISIS
of LIBERAL BELIEF

GEORGE M. MARSDEN

BASIC BOOKS

A MEMBER OF THE PERSEUS BOOKS GROUP

NEW YORK

Published by Basic Books,

A Member of the Perseus Books Group

Books published by Basic Books are available at special discounts for bulk purchases in the United States by corporations, institutions, and other organizations. For more information, please contact the Special Markets Department at the Perseus Books Group, 2300 Chestnut Street, Suite 200, Philadelphia, PA 19103, or call (800) 810-4145, ext. 5000, or e-mail special.markets@perseusbooks.com.

Typeset in Minion Pro by the Perseus Books Group

Library of Congress Cataloging-in-Publication Data
Marsden, George M., 1939–
     The twilight of the American enlightenment : the 1950s and the crisis of liberal belief / George M. Marsden.
          pages   cm
     Includes bibliographical references and index.
     ISBN 978-0-465-03010-1 (hardback)—ISBN 978-0-465-06977-4 (ebook) 1. United States—Civilization—1945– 2. United States—Social conditions—1945– 3. Cold War—Social aspects—United States. 4. Alienation (Social psychology)—United States—History—20th century. 5. Group identity—United States—History—20th century. I. Title.
     E169.12.M3647 2013
     973.91—dc23
     2013032100

10 9 8 7 6 5 4 3 2 1

To my former students,
with thanks for all they have done

Contents

Introduction

MANY AMERICANS THINK OF THE 1950S AS A TIME
when American culture made sense. Some of us can remember
why. We had won the war, we were enjoying unprecedented
prosperity, and we were surrounded by visible signs of progress. Comfortable suburbs sprang up everywhere. I remember
well how, in the spring of 1949, when I was ten years old, the
fields near my home where we used to roam were suddenly
marked off with patterns of stakes. A building project was
launched with some fanfare—the developers even gave away
aluminum horseshoe tokens with a 1949 penny in the center.
By the next spring, our town had a full-fledged suburb, where
I would soon be delivering newspapers. In such places, more
and more young families could participate in the American
dream of owning their own homes endowed with up-to-date
modern conveniences. Everyone seemed to take the ideal of the
conventional family for granted. The father went off to work,
and the mother dedicated herself to raising the children. Typically, the front yards on my paper route were littered with bicy-
cles and tricycles. For many people in the 1950s, an expanding
amount of free time could be dedicated to entertainment (a

small blue-gray TV flickered in most picture windows), leisure, and sports. Children and teenagers were among the chief
beneficiaries of these changes, enjoying a whole youth culture
of rock 'n' roll music, films, TV shows, comic books, sports,
and activities designed especially for them. Not everyone yet
shared in the American dream, of course, but the nation was
working on that. The society was becoming more and more
inclusive, and the people within it were increasingly sharing
similar values. Granted, a lot of problems remained to be
solved. Yet there was little reason not to believe that, if peace
could be maintained, progress would continue.

In many ways, the mid-twentieth century was a time of
tremendous optimism. Americans were constantly being reminded that theirs was the best nation on earth. They heard
every day that their happiness and contentment would only increase, particularly if they acquired the latest products. Probably no one quite believed all the hype, but still, in many ways,
things (and it was especially *things*) were better than they had
ever been. As Alan Ehrenhalt, author of *The Lost City*, put it
in that engaging look back at growing up in Chicago, it was
"not that the 1950s were a golden age . . . but that they were a
time when life as it was seemed so much better than life might
have been." Everyone could remember or had heard of endur-
ing the hardships of the Depression, or could look back to or
imagine coming of age in 1943, when boys were sent off to an
incredibly grim world war.

Ehrenhalt recalls especially "the forgotten virtues of community in America" that still prevailed in the 1950s. Most folks'
lives were shaped by the community of the neighborhood or

town in which they lived. Well-known local people typically owned and ran the stores that were part of that community. Even when families moved to the suburbs, they worked hard at creating a sense of togetherness through community organizations and churches. One of the dimensions of the urban neighborhoods was the presence of authority—sometimes arbitrary authority. That was especially true for those who lived in Catholic neighborhoods, where parish priests often ruled with an iron hand. Every child who attended a Catholic school could recall nuns whose lives seemed dedicated to being God's agent for enforcing discipline, order, and uniformity. In all these communities, Catholic and otherwise, the authoritarian father, easily angered by the laxness and indifference of the younger generation, was a figure everyone knew of either first or second hand. Yet according to Ehrenhalt, it is not just nostalgia to regard such occasionally strict authority as a fair price to pay for a sense of genuine community—a sense of community that has been lost for so many Americans of later eras that seem to be shaped by the "chaos of choice."[1]

It is easy to understand why many people today might wish for a return to the virtues of those seemingly simpler times. First of all, it is human nature to look back on an earlier era, especially the days of one's youth, as being more coherent than the disruptive times of later years. At least that has been the way it has looked to Euro-Americans ever since the 1660s, when Puritan preachers were contemplating an American-born generation and lamenting the decline from the days of the founders. For cultural conservatives today it is especially understandable to think of the 1950s as a time when traditional morality and religion were still respected in the cultural mainstream. *New York Times* columnist Ross Douthat has written fondly of the place that religion held in society during the Eisenhower years, when what Douthat has depicted as a sort of consensus Christian orthodoxy had wide influence in American public life. Certainly, there was more public respect for religion then than there is at present. In many public schools of the 1950s, days opened with the Pledge of Allegiance, a Bible reading, and the Lord's Prayer. Traditional Judeo-Christian standards, such as monogamous, heterosexual marriage, were the dominant public norms. Even some cultural liberals who today would not approve of the ideal of stay-at-home moms—or of censorship according to the Motion Picture Production Code—can celebrate "The Greatest Generation." That was, as Tom Brokaw famously described it, the World War II generation, the generation that came home from the war to apply "the same passions and disciplines that had served them so well in the war" to building "the most powerful peacetime economy in history" and to bringing stunning achievements in many fields.[2]

Understandable and even admirable as such regard for the accomplishments of our forebears is, we should at the same time recall that the 1950s were an era of great cultural anxiety and uncertainty. The most immediate anxieties arose in response to the combination of the Cold War and the Bomb. The United States, which had been traditionally isolationist, had been thrown into a position of world leadership. It faced a fearful totalitarian power and the possibility of a war that might obliterate civilization itself. Having fought two world wars within a generation, Americans feared World War III, which, even if most people tried not to think about it, seemed almost inevitable.

That much is well remembered, but far less recalled and reflected upon is another level of cultural crisis that is the point of departure for this book. For the most thoughtful observers of American life of the time, the most basic question was whether this civilization could be saved from itself. The horrors engineered by Adolf Hitler and other totalitarian dictators had demonstrated that Western civilization was in the midst of a profound crisis and that democracy was hardly a guarantee against barbarism. If the Holocaust could take place in Germany, one of the most advanced nations in the world both culturally and intellectually, what was to prevent such atrocities elsewhere? The forces of modernity itself might be destabilizing civilization. Evidence was abundant that the headlong rush from tradition to modernity was disorienting to "modern man," to repeat a widely used phrase of the day. Many observers worried that scientifically based authorities, such as those leading the new studies of psychology and the other social sciences, were destroying traditional religious and moral restraints. At the same time, modern technology was spawning mass culture and forms of entertainment that appealed to the lowest common denominator and offered a shallow and empty reality. Cultural analysts worried that people in modern mass cultures might be all too ready to give up their freedom for the false securities of totalitarian ideologies. Modern artists routinely depicted the emptiness and fragmentation of contemporary life. Writers portrayed figures such as the empty Willie

Loman in *Death of a Salesman* or the disillusioned Holden Caulfield in *Catcher in the Rye*. Movie titles such as *The Man in the Gray Flannel Suit* and *Rebel Without a Cause* captured the spirit of the age. More systematic observers reflected on themes such as "the lonely crowd," "the sane society," "the organization man," or "the status seekers."[3]

My own fascination with these cultural analyses began more than half a century ago when I was a college student in the late 1950s. They were my introductions to intriguing questions about how to understand the American civilization in which I had grown up. I decided to return to the topic when, in 2009, I was teaching a course at Harvard Divinity School on "Faith and Learning in American Culture," and I was struck once again by the way in which the characteristic assumptions of the 1950s regarding science and religion contributed to later problems. In particular, those assumptions helped impede the development of a fully inclusive pluralism in American academia and in American society generally. In revisiting the mainstream thought of the era, I hope to bring together perspectives shaped by my sense of both how this mainstream thought looked at the time and how it looks in the light of what has happened in the past half-century.

The chronology of decades is, of course, artificial. The dominant American cultural traits of "the 1950s" emerged shortly after World War II. Many of these traits persisted into the early 1960s, although the election of John F. Kennedy in 1960 provides a convenient marker for at least a change in mood. I use "the 1950s" as a term that is synonymous with this broader midcentury culture, although the vast majority of my examples come from within that decade.[4]

This book has three main themes or motifs. The first, which is most dominant in Chapters 1 and 2, is a recounting of how American culture looked through the eyes of the most perceptive and highly regarded cultural analysts of the time. What were its greatest challenges? In what did they place their hopes? What were the assumptions that these mainstream analysts could take for granted? These questions lead to the second and central motif, which is most explicit in Chapters 3 and 4 but echoes throughout the whole. That is the notion that the typical consensus outlooks of the time can be understood as attempts to preserve the ideals of the American enlightenment while discarding its foundations. The culminating motif, developed in Chapters 5 and 6 as well as the Conclusion, relates these themes to the role of religion in American public life both in the 1950s and since then up to the present.

Concerning the first motif, two things become particularly striking when we look back at what the leading public intellectuals of the mid-twentieth century had to say about the state of American civilization and, more broadly, Western civilization. The first is the perceptiveness of some of their insights into the modern predicament. They were reflecting on some breathtaking changes in the human experience, many of which had taken place in their own lifetimes. Midcentury observers, viewing so many innovations—such as car and air travel, electronic mass communications, mass production, household appliances, modern weaponry, efficient police states, modern medicine, and dependence on psychology and other scientific experts (to name just a few)—in the light of the well-remembered practices and outlooks they replaced, were especially attuned to the larger significance of these changes for the state of civilization. By contrast, most of us take many of the features of modernity for granted; we continue to experience rapid technological change, but we have grown accustomed to the pace. We can benefit today from the reflections of those from an earlier era—an era in which modern times were new.

The second striking feature is the contrast between the perceptiveness of their diagnoses and the inadequacies of their prescriptions. Looking back on even the wisest of these observers, we have the advantage of knowing what they could not have known: that the whole concept of "American civilization" (and even the more fundamental "Western civilization") and their place within it was about to change dramatically. These moderate-liberal thinkers, who stood near the center of the cultural establishment, were living in the last days before a cultural revolution. Although they had no idea what was coming, they were correct in identifying a deep crisis regarding the quality of their civilization. They in fact anticipated some of the complaints that young people would take to the streets in the later 1960s. Yet, in retrospect, we can see that they had no solutions beyond more of the same. Their responses to the perceived emptiness of much of modern life typically amounted to shoring up the levees of the consensus culture, and these levees were wildly inadequate for holding back the floodwaters of cultural upheaval that were about to crash against them.

Trying to recapture a sense of how American civilization looked to its own leading analysts during these last days before the cultural revolution of the late twentieth century is an intriguing process in itself, as is any imaginative journey into a lost era. As a guide on this journey I point out only some "must-see" highlights, rather than offering a thorough scholarly analysis. I am not writing for specialists who concentrate on the thought of elite intellectuals. Instead, I want to help the general reader imagine how the cultural crisis and prospects of the day might have looked to the informed layperson of the 1950s, someone who was part of what was then called the "middlebrow" audience of those who kept an eye on accessible cultural analysis in books, magazines, and reviews.

In choosing to reconstruct this one aspect of the 1950s outlook, I realize that there are many important and fascinating features of the era that I am not getting into except as context. One might elaborate, for example, on some of the same themes examined here, especially themes of cultural critique, in the fiction, plays, and films of the era. Popular culture, from Lucy to Elvis, or from *Ladies Home Journal* to *Esquire*, tells some different stories. Much has been written about the 1950s, and the decade is still often depicted in pop culture—for example, in the television series *Mad Men*, or in other shows, films, and books that invoke standardized suburban life and the typical gender roles of the times. Or, on another note, people in the 1950s worried over seemingly rampant juvenile delinquency. The politics of the era tells a number of different stories, about the Cold War, Korea, McCarthyism, and early civil rights. The 1950s was the era of the birth of a self-conscious and intellectualized conservative movement, as represented by Russell Kirk, William F. Buckley, and Ayn Rand. For the economy, it was a time of immense business and technological growth and an unprecedented consumer-driven prosperity.

Features of the 1950s such as these provided the context for the public conversations regarding the quality and the future of American civilization that is our main focus. Most of the participants in this discussion were white male journalists and public intellectuals who commanded considerable middlebrow readership. That such cultural leadership was primarily a male activity was as much taken for granted as that "man" was the correct inclusive pronoun. Nonetheless, as had been true since the days of Harriet Beecher Stowe, outstanding women could be admitted to the club. Traditionally, cultural leaders had been overwhelmingly Protestant, at least in heritage, although recently the club doors had been flung open to include a striking number of Jews, who took leading roles in much of the conversation. The question of whether Western civilization, under American leadership, could survive in the wake of the cultural trends that had led to the Holocaust was self-evidently a most urgent question for Jews, and the broader middlebrow readership proved ready to listen. Catholics, by contrast, only rarely gained a voice in the cultural mainstream prior to the eve of the Kennedy era.

Most of the conversation emanated from the Northeast, to some extent from New England but more often from New York, which was unrivaled as the nation's cultural center. The participants in the mainstream were, broadly speaking, "liberal."

"Who the hell are you not to be a liberal?"

Frank Model, March 18, 1950, *The New Yorker*

Although that term had no precise meaning at the time, in general it meant centrist: one who was neither leftist (many American intellectuals had flirted with Marxism in the 1930s, but had since repented) nor "conservative." The most evident threat to America was the vast Soviet empire, which in its ugly Stalinist form made a consensus of liberal opposition easy to establish. The prominent literary scholar Lionel Trilling went so far as to say in 1950 that "liberalism is not only the dominant but even the sole intellectual tradition in America," a view that gained wide assent among moderate thinkers of the day. Sometimes I refer to them as "moderate-liberal" in order to signal that I am describing a broadly shared outlook rather than any precise ideology. Whether they were Republican or (more often) Democrat, they could participate in a single national conversation based on a broadly "liberal" consensus. Their job, as they saw it, was to define on that basis where

American civilization was, and then to provide guidance as to where it should be headed.[5]

ONE OF THE MOST FASCINATING and helpful dimensions of understanding another era comes about through the process of teasing out its widely shared underlying assumptions. The dominant public conversations of each age and culture have their characteristic, shared, taken-for-granted beliefs. Certain ideals or authoritative principles can be asserted without need for real argument in any age. At the time, they may seem almost self-evident, but later generations may find them curious. Not that later outlooks are necessarily better. Rather, we should recognize that dominant outlooks may improve in some respects while the society simultaneously loses some of the wisdom or insights of the past. Nonetheless, with that reminder, we can ask about the 1950s what assumptions were widely taken for granted that might seem peculiar or questionable to most observers today.

That question brings us to the second motif and the central interpretive argument of the book, developed most in the middle two chapters: that the underlying assumptions of the dominant outlooks of the 1950s can be better understood if we think of them as latter-day efforts to sustain the ends of the American enlightenment, but without that enlightenment's intellectual means. Since the word "enlightenment" as a historical term is used in many different ways, I hasten to add that I am not using it in any technical or philosophical sense. For example, I am not using it as it was used by some European-oriented intellectuals at the time, or as it has been used by some postmodernists in more recent years.[6] Instead, I am using it in a sense that can be easily understood in a layperson's terms: as referring to the characteristic outlook of the eighteenth-century American founders. My argument is that the mainstream thinkers of the 1950s can be better understood if we see them as standing in far more continuity with the cultural assumptions of the founders than would be true of most mainstream thinkers today. At the same time, the discontinuities between their assumptions and those of the founders were formidable. Consequently, their hopes for providing a common ground for a cultural consensus could not be long sustained.

The American founders, men such as Benjamin Franklin, Thomas Jefferson, George Washington, John Adams, James Madison, and the like, took for granted that there was a Creator who established natural laws, including moral laws, that could be known to humans as self-evident principles to be understood and elaborated through reason. Most mainstream mid-twentieth-century American thinkers, who, like most modern thinkers, assumed collective intellectual progress, thought of themselves as having left such eighteenth-century enlightenment views behind. They were post-Darwinists who worked in a framework in which they took for granted human evolution and cultural evolution that shaped human beliefs and mores. They believed that societies developed their own laws, rather than discovering them in the fixed order of things. Yet, despite their modernized intellectual starting points, many of their fundamental assumptions and goals were very much in continuity with those of America's enlightened founders. They took for granted as self-evident many of the founders' assumptions regarding human freedom, self-determination, and equality of rights. In fact, their hopes for strengthening the American "consensus" were built around the faith that America could be united on the basis of these evolving shared ideals. They also shared with eighteenth-century leaders a confidence that rational and scientific understandings were essentially objective and therefore should be normative. Most of them believed that applying natural scientific methods and empirically based rationality to understanding society was one of the best ways to promote human flourishing. In addition, they often celebrated the "autonomous" individual, an ideal that Benjamin Franklin, for instance, would have approved. So, despite the erosion of the original premises on which the enlightenment hopes had been built, the mid-twentieth-century thinkers shared the essentials of that hope. That outlook, especially its reverence for science and the individual, was commonplace in popular and commercial culture as well.

One of the most conspicuous continuity with the eighteenth century and discontinuity with the twenty-first century was in assumptions regarding male leadership. In the eighteenth century, "the rights of men" had meant quite literally the rights of males. By the 1950s women were included, in principle. Yet, in practice, when it came to cultural leadership, almost everyone, including most women, assumed that men would predominate. Outstanding women were welcomed here and there, but as exceptions to an assumed rule.

In practice, cultural leadership was also almost entirely the prerogative of white men, but in the case of race, the continuities with the American enlightenment had an important positive effect. Race prejudice and the power of slaveholders had prevented the founders from extending the full logic of the "rights of man" to African Americans. In the 1950s, the nation was still sharply divided on that score, especially, but by no means exclusively, North and South. But most mainstream intellectuals of the moderate-liberal variety favored full equality among the races. They wished to bring the enlightenment logic of the founders to its proper conclusion.

In speaking of this dominant midcentury outlook as representing a latter-day version of the faith and hope of the American enlightenment, it is essential to be reminded of the significant place of Protestant Christianity in the American enlightenment. Unlike the French enlightenment and the French Revolution, the American Revolution involved a cordial working relationship between the dominant religious groups and most enlightened ways of thinking. In fact, a distinctive feature of the American experience was the synthesis of Protestant and enlightenment principles that one finds widely in the early republic. The colonies were overwhelmingly Protestant by heritage, and so Protestant support was of a piece with the revolutionary effort. Protestantism, even then, came in many varieties, from evangelical to liberal to deist and nominal, but almost all of these proved adaptable to prevailing eighteenth-century enlightened British and American assumptions. Typically, the proponents of all these forms of Protestantism saw a high regard for natural science, reason, common sense, self-evident rights, and ideals of liberty as fully compatible with their Protestant heritage. The more orthodox usually saw the truths of reason and nature and the higher truths of faith and revelation as simply complementary. More liberal Protestants, of whom Jefferson was a prototype, had greater faith in the dictates of reason as the standard that would shape the religion of the future. Despite such differences, by the early decades of the nineteenth century, mainstream American thought, as seen, for instance, in what was taught at most colleges, was a fusion of varieties of Protestantism with various degrees of enlightenment regard for natural science, reason, and commonsense moral judgments. Almost everyone agreed that Protestant Christianity provided an important support for the principles upon which the republic had been founded.[7]

Between the mid-nineteenth century and the mid-twentieth, this fusion of Protestant and more secular principles went through a number of permutations in response to romanticism, Darwinism, pragmatism, the rise of social sciences, and a dramatic liberalization of much of mainline Protestantism (that is, the major predominantly northern denominations, such as Episcopal, Congregational, Presbyterian, Baptist, Methodist, Lutheran, and others), but something like the old alliance was still perceptible in the 1950s.[8]

The overall cultural arrangements thus remained in continuity with the American enlightenment, particularly in the hope that a coalition of cultural leaders, including some religious leaders, despite their differences, could somehow guide the society toward a progressive, enlightened, and humane cultural consensus. Nobody thought that it would be an easy project. The founding fathers had realized that building a coherent voluntary civilization out of many competing subgroups would involve a tremendous balancing act. Mid-twentieth-century leaders wrestled with American ethnic, religious, and racial diversity, the disruptions of modernity and mass culture. The immensely precarious world scene increased the difficulties and raised the stakes. Extreme McCarthyite anticommunism, anti-intellectualism, populist racism, fundamentalist religion, and just the sheer shallowness of American commercialism and popular culture made it evident that the challenges were formidable. America had been thrust into world leadership, and this role accentuated the urgency of articulating ideals that would not only help bring unity out of diversity at home, but prove worthy of respect abroad.

THIS BRINGS US TO THE culminating motif of the book: reflections on the implications of this history for understanding the role of a variety of religions in American culture both in the 1950s and since. This theme predominates in Chapters 5 and 6 and in the Conclusion.

The starting point for this exploration is a look at the role of the Protestant establishment in the consensus culture of the 1950s. Even though the vast majority of cultural analysis at midcentury was conducted in thoroughly secular terms, liberal Protestants retained a respected place in the cultural mainstream. Christianity, properly understood, and natural science, properly understood, the analysts typically argued, were not at odds. Rather, truths of faith and truths of science were complementary in that they dealt with two different realms of human experience. On such a basis, Protestant theologians, of whom Reinhold Niebuhr was the best known, could be prominent voices within the liberal mainstream. In Niebuhr's case, his chastening words regarding the human condition could be welcomed, but his generalized Christianity offered little to challenge most of the secularizing trends that he himself identified.

When the consensus culture collapsed in the 1960s and 1970s, taking with it all but the vestiges of the old Protestant establishment, that collapse initiated, among other things, a religious crisis.[9] Formal recognition of Christianity, as in public school prayers and observances, declined at the same time. There were tumultuous changes in mores and a questioning of the shared patriotism that had characterized the 1940s and 1950s. This combination led at first to a cultural backlash, and then, by the later 1970s, to the rise of the religious right and the initiation of the culture wars. Although I do not attempt a full account of these developments here, I do offer an overview to illustrate how they may be illuminated by viewing them in the context of the demise of the consensus culture of the 1950s and the rise of the idea of taking back America by restoring a lost "Christian consensus."

These observations on the 1950s consensus outlook and the subsequent rise of the culture wars lead to the constructive purpose of this book, made explicit in the Conclusion, which is to reflect upon the problem of how American public life might better accommodate religious pluralism. My argument, in brief, is that the culture wars broke out and persisted in part because the dominant principles of the American heritage did not adequately provide for how to deal with substantive religious differences as they relate to the public domain.

The American paradigm for relating religion to public life was an unusual blend of enlightenment and Protestant ideals. In some ways it was the model of inclusivism and religious freedom. But because it also fostered an informal Protestant establishment, or privileges for mainstream Protestants in public life, there were always those who were less privileged, who were excluded or discriminated against—such as Catholics, Jews, people of other world faiths, or those in smaller sectarian groups. Even in the more inclusive 1950s, mainstream Protestantism retained its preeminence in American public life. It is not surprising then that, by the 1970s, after the long-standing enlightenment-Protestant paradigm collapsed, mainstream America lacked the theoretical resources for constructing a more truly pluralistic way of dealing with the relationships of varieties of religions to public life. My contribution is to point to an alternative paradigm for thinking about the varieties of religious outlooks in the public sphere and the roles they play within that sphere.

Finally, let me say a word about point of view. One of the conventions of the mid-twentieth century was that authors and teachers normally did not identify their points of view but spoke as though they were neutral observers speaking on the basis of universal reason. Such practices reflected standards that went back to the eighteenth-century enlightenment, in which one was to hold forth on most topics on the basis of objective standards rather than from the point of view of one's particular faith. Mid-twentieth-century commentators, unless they belonged to a peculiar party or sect, could speak as though they represented an outlook that, at least so far as fundamental assumptions were concerned, every educated person should share. Every critical thinker recognized, of course, that their opponents at least were smuggling in some biases. But even those who recognized the relativism inherent in much of modern thought rarely spelled out exactly what their own prejudices might be. Such conventions of discourse in fact helped to create the illusion that it was still possible to create a national consensus, despite residual sectarian differences.

In recent decades there has been greater recognition that, although there are common standards for rational discourse, arguments, and evidence, there is no one standard, underlying set of assumptions, including beliefs about the ultimate nature of reality and values, that all rational educated people can somehow be presumed to share. So, although many still follow the old convention of posing as though one were objective, it has become more acceptable these days to help out the reader or listener by identifying one's fundamental viewpoint from the outset.

My own point of view has been shaped most basically by my commitments as an Augustinian Christian.[10] Those commitments involve a recognition that people differ in their fundamental loves and first principles, and that these loves and first principles act as lenses through which they see everything else. At the same time, all humans, as fellow creatures of God, share many beliefs in common and can communicate through common standards of rational discourse. Furthermore, even though I am an Augustinian Christian, I am also shaped in part by many other beliefs and commitments that have been common in America in the twentieth and twenty-first centuries. One of my goals in life has been to understand such characteristic American beliefs and to critically and constructively relate them to my religious beliefs. This book is an instance of that project. Much of it is about understanding a fascinating moment of the American experience, but that account leads to critical analysis and reflection on the question of the place that religion should have in that culture.

I hope that readers who hold other points of view, whether secular or religious, can nonetheless learn from what I present here. Although I write from a specific point of view, I do not differ from other writers or public intellectuals in that respect; I differ only in that I identify my viewpoint more explicitly than some of these other writers do. I hope that readers will benefit from that identification. It may allow them to learn from my analysis while taking into account the parts of my perspective with which they do not agree. That frank recognition of differences may then help them to better appreciate the understandings and insights that we can hold in common.

Prologue
The National Purpose

IN THE LATE SPRING OF 1960, *LIFE*, AMERICA'S IMMENSELY popular pictorial newsmagazine, claiming a readership of 25 million, published a "crucial U.S. debate" in a five-part series on "The National Purpose." The authors, a distinguished group, included not only professional observers of the national scene, headed by the legendary Walter Lippmann, but also men of practical affairs, such as David Sarnoff, head of the Radio Corporation of America. Others, such as poet Archibald MacLeish, recent two-time Democratic presidential candidate Adlai Stevenson, and evangelist Billy Graham, were among the most famous representatives of major areas of American life. It was unremarkable at the time that all the contributors were white males. It was just as unremarkable that the forum included a clergyman, even though the clergyman was an ardent evangelical (as well as being the only southerner in the mix).[1]

Henry R. Luce, editor-in-chief of *Life*, explained in his foreword to the book version, which appeared later in the year, that, "more than anything else, the people of America are asking for a clear sense of National Purpose." Providing a sort of

Norman Rockwell touch, he wrote that "a group of citizens may begin by talking about the price of eggs or the merits of education, but they end by asking each other: what are we trying to do overall? Where are we trying to get? What is the National Purpose of the U.S.A.?" America had become "the greatest nation in the world." But the questions of the day were about what America would now "*do* with the greatness" and whether it was "great in the right way."

Luce was one of the most influential opinion shapers in America, perhaps *the* most influential for the rank and file of the reading public. He was the head of a publishing empire that included not only *Life* but also *Time* (the most widely read print newsmagazine in the country in an era when print still held its place as the most respected medium), *Fortune* (the leading business weekly), and the new *Sports Illustrated*. Luce, a Yale graduate and the son of Presbyterian missionaries to China, was a wide-ranging and inventive thinker in his own right. America was his mission, and he tended to see the interests of God and country as going hand in hand. He invented the phrase "The American Century" in 1941, having prophesied prior to America's entry into the war that the nation was destined to become the leader of the free world. Americans had taken up that task and warmed to it. Now, almost twenty years later, the nation seemed to be drifting, and Luce wished to clarify where it should be heading.

The immediate context was that 1960 was an election year, and it was not clear exactly where the nation was headed. The recent years had been the first in a generation when the nation's purpose had not been clear. In the 1930s, the nation had the clear goal of recovering from the Depression. Then came World War II, postwar rebuilding, and the Korean War. Ike had been president since 1953. He had led the "Crusade in Europe," as he had titled his World War II memoir in 1948, but his presidency had been marked by his efforts to fend off the efforts of others to create a crusading or crisis atmosphere. Early in his presidency he had faced a challenge led by Senator Joseph McCarthy, who had attempted to turn anticommunism into a major domestic purge of anyone who had ever had left-ist affiliations. The Cold War was at its height, and one of Ike's goals was to dampen the kind of zealotry that might lead to World War III. Moderation, however, came at a price: it could seem like lack of direction. Ever since the Soviet Union had launched its Sputnik satellite in 1957, critics of the administration had complained of a missile gap, saying that America was losing the space race. On the domestic front, there was a great deal of anxiety as to whether unprecedented prosperity and shallow popular culture might be causing the nation to lose its moral bearings as well.

In the original *Life* version of the series, the magazine's chief editorial writer, John K. Jessup (Yale '28), set the stage for the discussion. Amid lavish color illustrations of national icons, Jessup guided readers through the high points of American rhetoric, from the Declaration of Independence to Franklin D. Roosevelt. The American project of building democracy had become, as Woodrow Wilson had declared, an international project of "making the world safe for democracy." Yet the Cold War world of the 1950s seemed anything but safe, and Americans seemed to be faltering on sustaining the first

"The state the world's in, Polly, all I'm planting is annuals."

James Stevenson, April 30, 1960, *The New Yorker*

principles upon which democracy was built. "Self-government" had been a perennial American goal, he said, but today that idea, "that men can govern themselves in freedom under law," might seem "too 18th Century for the world's needs today, or America's complex relation to it." Furthermore, Jessup argued, "democracy . . . is not the highest value known to man." Rather, it works only because it is grounded in "higher allegiances," allegiances, that is, to "moral law." Americans, he affirmed, have a "public love affair with righteousness," because "our very right of self-government is derived from 'the Laws of Nature and of Nature's God.'" If Americans were to answer communism around the world in an effective way, then they ought to be able to provide a new articulation of John Locke and the founding fathers' principle that freedom is grounded in rights to property. But Jessup recognized that Americans had lost such a clear sense of purpose. He quoted a letter from a US Air Force lieutenant to *Time*: "What America stands for is making money, and as the society approaches affluence, its members are left to stew in their own ennui."

Most of the other eight contributors to the *Life* series expressed concern that something like the lieutenant's views represented the national mood, or even the reality, all too well. Walter Lippmann, who had just turned seventy and was still widely regarded as America's wisest commentator, had been one of the most influential voices in saying America had lost its sense of purpose. Part of the problem, said Lippmann, was that earlier national purposes had been fulfilled. "We have reached a point," he wrote, "in our internal development and in our relations with the rest of the world where we have fulfilled and outlived most of what we used to regard as the program of our national purposes." The nation was like a man who had set out to cross the continent from New York and had gotten to Chicago, but was not sure which route ought to be taken from there.

Always one to keep the big picture in mind, Lippmann observed that "in the 15 years which have passed since the end of the second World War, the condition of mankind has changed more rapidly and more deeply than in any other period within the experience of the American people." Among the most worrisome problems were world population growth, "a great and threatening agglomeration of people in cities," and a "swift and radical change in the balance of power" that might foster worldwide revolutions. At the same time, people everywhere were experiencing "radical change in the technology of war and in the technology of industry." The ever-present threat of the obliteration by the bomb immensely raised the stakes in the discussion. On the home front, technology had changed almost every aspect of life. The advent of new mass media was particularly momentous, he said, "because it marks a revolution in popular education and in the presentation of information, and in the very nature of debate and deliberation." It was thereby profoundly altering the assumptions on which a democratic society might be built.

Historian Clinton Rossiter framed the problem much as Lippmann did, suggesting that America was suffering from lost glory. "In our youth," said Rossiter, "we had a profound sense of national purpose, which we lost over the years of our rise to glory." Our "youthful sense of mission" was "in fact fulfilled nobly." One only had to look at all the constitutional democracies in the world to see the truth of this claim. Now, however, America had become middle aged, Rossiter observed; striking a chord that resonated throughout the series, he added, "We are fat and complacent." Whereas once we were a people "on the make," now we were a people who "'has it made,' and we find it hard to rouse to the trumpet of sacrifice—even if anyone in authority were to blow it."

John Gardner, president of the Carnegie Foundation, did not think Americans had lost their ideals, but nonetheless conceded that there was "a danger of losing our bearings," and that "part of our problem is how to stay awake on a full stomach." The distinguished poet and playwright Archibald MacLeish saw the crisis as more deeply rooted, but he agreed that Americans still had a sense of purpose. "That something has gone wrong in America," he began, "most of us know." The problem was our riches. "We have more Things in our garages and kitchens and cellars than Louis Quatorze had in the whole of Versailles." Yet, despite "the materialism about which we talk so much," our unease with it was a sign of hope. That was true especially among the "intelligent young," whose current favorite whipping boys were the Madison Avenue ad men, who were said to "persuade us to wallow in cosmetics and tail-fin cars." MacLeish added presciently, "We may be drowning in Things, but the best of our sons and daughters like it even less than we do."

Billy Graham warned that the nation's flaws were potentially fatal, and he challenged the widespread view that the problems might be self-correcting. America, he began, was like a man with whom he had played golf a few months earlier, who had appeared to be healthy, but since had died of cancer. In the midst of affluence, "America is said to have the highest per capita boredom of any spot on earth." That emptiness was reflected in youth culture in which "rebels without a cause" were rebelling from conformity for the sake of rebelling. Only change from the inside out, or Christian conversion, could transform people in the way that was necessary to renew the culture. Then Americans could recapture their individualism, patriotism, discipline, and courage, qualities that had "made us the greatest nation in the world." Ultimately, though, America's strength must be used for altruistic ends. The nation must share its wealth, said Graham. It should attack "the worldwide problems of ignorance, disease and poverty."

One of the most striking features of the series was how many of the authors worried that Americans' self-indulgent materialism might be making them unfit to be leaders of the free world in the fight against communism. That fight, after all, provided the most urgent context for the anxieties over national purpose. Graham quoted the famed diplomat George Kennan to make the point that a country "with no highly developed sense of national purpose, with the overwhelming accent of life on personal comfort, with a dearth of public services and a surfeit of privately sold gadgetry" could simply not compete with the Soviet Union. Adlai Stevenson quipped, "With the supermarket as our temple and the singing commercial as our litany, are we likely to fire the world with an irresistible vision of America's exalted purposes and inspiring way of life?"

In offering solutions, most of the authors agreed that the national ideals themselves were adequate and that there was no easy fix for the perils of prosperity, but that what was needed was a sort of pragmatism that would rely on practical problem-solving rather than on grand ideological abstractions. Clinton Rossiter argued that in the face of the nuclear threat "it has now become the destiny of this nation to lead the world prudently and pragmatically" toward a world "government having power to enforce peace." Albert Wohlstetter, of the Rand Corporation, the one scientist in the group, who had recently been scientific adviser in arms talks with the Soviets, was skeptical of the talk about "national purpose," because there were multiple purposes. For example, the nation needed both economic growth and nuclear deterrence. Wohlstetter went on to show how these two objectives could be compatible. James "Scotty" Reston, whose *New York Times* editorial on the topic was added to the original nine in the book version, best stated the need for the primacy of pragmatism, saying, "If George Washington had waited for the doubters to develop a sense of purpose in the 18th century, he'd still be crossing the Delaware." Reston proclaimed that he was "all for self-direction and self criticism," but in fact believed it was more urgent to address the nation's practical problems. America still had the ideals and resources it needed to solve them. Things got done with effective leaders. And the upcoming election, he reminded everyone, would provide the country with the opportunity to find such a leader.

ONE

Mass Media and the
National Character

The *LIFE* MAGAZINE SYMPOSIUM ON "THE NATIONAL Purpose" exemplifies a well-remembered feature of the 1950s: the effort to build a national consensus in the face of the Communist threat. Adlai Stevenson and Billy Graham could bat in the same lineup. They, along with business leaders, journalists, scientists, and other scholars, could join in a single national conversation. Looking back, we may be more likely to notice those who were left out, but at the time it seemed that leaders from many areas of American life, as well as most of the rank and file, were at least standing on common ground. Despite ominous fault lines and sharp differences about specifics, they seemed to find enough common ground, formed by shared "American" assumptions, to talk meaningfully together about "our" heritage. In fact, the degree of public consensus in the 1950s, whatever its limits, distinguishes the era from many other times, before and especially since.

At the same time, one of the areas of agreement revealed by such discussions was that there was a lot to worry about regarding the quality of American civilization. For instance, one of the recurrent themes in the *Life* series was the danger that prosperity and new technology might lead to moral erosion of the national character. This danger was a much-discussed anxiety of the day. The nation's wealth was a major source of America's strength as a bastion against the Soviet Union. But analysts of the nation's character seemed to agree both that material strength was not sufficient in itself and that unprecedented prosperity might be loaded with unprecedented perils.

The danger of new riches was an old story, but the best cultural observers of the 1950s interpreted that story with a modern twist. The next two chapters recount some of that analysis in order to provide a sense of the characteristic outlooks and assumptions of the times. These ways of thinking about American civilization differed in some significant ways from most thinking about the same topic today. For one thing, mainstream commentators widely agreed that for America to flourish it was essential for it to carry forward whatever was the best of a highly valued heritage of "Western civilization." They also thought of the challenges to American civilization in terms of the recent crisis and near collapse of Western civilization and the rise of totalitarianism. America stood for democracy, but democracy in the twentieth-century world had proved alarmingly fragile. The United States was also hypermodern, and with all its new mass-produced technologies it seemed more modern by the month. Yet, since World War II, this hypermodern nation had been thrust into the position of

Garrett Price, September 3, 1955, *The New Yorker*

being the chief guardian of the Western "free world." A natural question to ask was whether there was something about the forces of modernity that might undermine something about the character of a citizenry that was necessary to sustain a free and healthy society.

Nothing elicited so much concern about the possible threats of modern technology to the quality of civilization as did the sudden advent of television. In 1947, most Americans had seen television only in store windows. By 1954, as many as 50 million people had watched some episodes of *I Love Lucy*. Suddenly television was dictating how most people spent their leisure time. In part because TV was dominated by the three almost identical national networks, it was creating a common culture to a greater extent than even radio and the movies had in previous decades. In the 1950s, more than in any era before or since, most Americans were watching the same things. The worry was that the culture of television was nationwide but an inch deep. TV seemed to have a mindlessness of its own.

The responses of leading American cultural observers to this perceived crisis offer a window into the time. The rise of television was part of the larger phenomenon of mass media, including radio, film, and mass-marketed print, that already had been reshaping twentieth-century life. But the abruptness of the TV revolution and its revolutionizing impact in changing the lives of almost everyone in the country was something that demanded reflection. These reflections provide a sense of how the media revolution looked at the time. They also reveal some of the common assumptions of the era, particularly the assumptions of public intellectuals, academics, and artists.

The sophisticated analysts were by no means alone in worrying that television was contributing to erosion of the national character. Late in the decade almost everyone seemed to join in as a media frenzy erupted over what might otherwise have been considered a fairly harmless TV misdemeanor. In 1955, CBS launched a new quiz show, *The $64,000 Question*, based on offering what at the time were enormous cash prizes to the contestants who survived the many rounds and weeks of questioning. The program soon gained nearly 50 million viewers, and the other networks followed suit with various imitations. For the next several years, these shows continued to garner huge audiences. But evidence was accumulating that the shows were rigged, and that contestants were routinely being prepped on their answers. By 1958, the story had become a national sensation. Rather than dismissing the manipulation as just "show business," the press covered it as a major national scandal that reflected something wrong at the heart of the culture. One participant later compared the coverage to that of the Watergate scandals of the 1970s.

By 1959, the investigations had been taken over by a congressional committee, and in November of that year the inquiry reached a dramatic climax: Charles Van Doren, the most popular and most respected of the contestants, confessed that he was indeed guilty of receiving prior answers. Many others were involved, but it was the corruption of Charles Van Doren that created by far the greatest consternation. His guilt was widely seen as symbolic of how deeply corruption had struck into the heart of the culture. Van Doren was not a greedy small-time operator off the street. The soft-spoken and winsome young man was from one of the leading literary families in the nation. His father, Mark Van Doren, a revered teacher at Columbia, had won a Pulitzer Prize, as had his uncle Carl. The young Van Doren, an instructor at Columbia himself, was highly educated in the best of the Western cultural heritage—a heritage that was supposed to be the antidote to the tawdry shallowness of popular culture.[1]

Leading cultural figures joined in the outcry, charging that America was losing its moral character. A striking instance was the reaction of novelist John Steinbeck. After nine months of working on a new book at a secluded English cottage, Steinbeck had just returned to America in November 1959 when the Van Doren story was at its height. In disgust, he wrote to his friend Adlai Stevenson that, "if I wanted to destroy a nation, I would give it too much and I would have it on its knees, miserable, greedy, and sick." The Van Doren scandal only verified how far the national corruption might reach. "On all levels," Steinbeck wrote, the society was "rigged" and riddled with "cynical immorality." The letter was published, "inadvertently," said Steinbeck, in the Long Island newspaper *Newsday*. It soon became fuel on the fires of the national conversation about what was going wrong with American civilization. Specifically, it triggered a symposium in *The New Republic* on the topic, entitled "Have We Gone Soft?" The all-male cast of commentators included such luminaries as Reinhold Niebuhr and Arthur Schlesinger Jr. Their reflections appeared in February 1960, just a few months before *Life* was to launch its more positively framed forum, but with the same subtext, on "The National Purpose."[2]

One reason that a few rigged TV shows could set off such an outpouring of national anxiety was that many people worried that the scandal was just the tip of a media iceberg that might be numbing the nation's collective moral sensibilities. If what passed for culture in America was increasingly to be dominated by TV, then what hope was there to cultivate the higher ideals necessary for the survival of Western civilization?

To appreciate such concerns one only has to look up the TV schedules of the day. For instance, the 1959–1960 primetime weekly lineup on the three national networks included more than a dozen westerns (*Gunsmoke*, *Bonanza*, *Have Gun Will Travel*, *Wyatt Earp*, *Tales of Wells Fargo*, *Wagon Train*, *Maverick*, *The Lawman*, *The Rifleman*, *Cheyenne*, *Wichita Town*, *Black Saddle*, and *Rawhide*), all with predictable moralistic plots. Alternatives on a typical evening included an assortment of crime and mystery shows (also mindless, except for

Alfred Hitchcock Presents), variety shows (hosted by Ed Sullivan, Danny Thomas, Red Skelton, Perry Como, and the like), quiz shows, and sitcoms such as *Leave It to Beaver, Ozzie and Harriet*, and *Father Knows Best*. In the earlier part of the decade, there had been a hope that television would be a means by which higher culture could be brought to the masses. Many had thought that the best of the theater could be adapted to the medium. By 1959–1960, all that was left of that ambitious idea were *Armstrong Circle Theater* and *Playhouse 90*, shown on Wednesday and Thursday nights, respectively. Serious theater had not proven sufficiently popular, and critics of television saw the surviving adaptations as mediocre debasements that were part of the problem, rather than the cure.[3]

The best known of the critics of TV and the mass media generally was Dwight Macdonald. A WASP purebred (Exeter and Yale), Macdonald had become prominent among New York intellectuals. Like many of his generation, he had gone through a Marxist stage in the 1930s before becoming staunchly anti-Communist in reaction to Stalinism. In a much-cited 1953 essay, Macdonald argued that popular culture was the new opiate of the masses in a capitalist society inexorably driven by the profit motive. (In the Soviet Union, the effect of mass media was similar, but the mind control was cruder and more direct than it was in the West.) According to Macdonald, *kitsch* (from the German term for popular but inferior art) and high culture could not simply coexist. Rather, in a capitalistic society, mass culture inevitably had a parasitic relationship with high culture. Driven as it was by the market and the profit motive, mass culture would overwhelm good taste. There was a "Gresham's Law in culture," as in monetary circulation, dictating that "bad stuff drives out the good, since it is easily understood and enjoyed."

Mass culture was inevitably degrading, said Macdonald, because, unlike folk art, it did not arise from the people but was manufactured and distributed from the top down. Often it would appropriate some of the characteristics of high culture and produce a "tepid flaccid Middlebrow Culture that threatens to engulf everything in its spreading ooze." It was also exceedingly democratic. Like nineteenth-century capitalism, "mass culture is a dynamic, revolutionary force, breaking down the old barriers of class, tradition, taste, and dissolving all cultural distinction." The result was a "homogenized" culture where everything was mixed together indiscriminately. *Life* magazine, Macdonald said, offered the perfect illustration of the problem. (One of Macdonald's first jobs had been working for fellow Yale alumnus Henry Luce.) *Life* could be found "on the mahogany library tables of the rich" and "the oilcloth-covered kitchen tables of the poor." It had something for everyone. Its cover might announce, in the same size type, "A NEW FOREIGN POLICY, BY JOHN FOSTER DULLES," and "KERIMA; HER MARATHON KISS IS A MOVIE SENSATION." Or it might have "nine color pages of Renoirs plus a memoir by his son, followed by a full-page picture of a horse on roller skates."

The problem, however, was not just slick magazines, bad television, too many adults reading comic books, or anything else that could be easily corrected by raising cultural standards and supporting the arts. Instead, it was that the whole character of the human race was being altered by the revolutionary force of the masses. "The masses are in historical time," Macdonald declared, "what a crowd is in space: a large quantity of people unable to express themselves as human beings" because they are "not related *to each other* at all, but only to something distant, abstract, nonhuman." They were no longer really a community or a folk or a people in whom there could be a healthy combination of individualism and community, which is conducive to great art. Rather, "a mass society, like a crowd, is so undifferentiated and loosely structured that its atoms, in so far as human values go, tend to cohere only along the line of the least common denominator; its morality sinks to that of its most brutal and primitive members, its taste to that of the least sensitive and most ignorant." Yet it was to that "collective monstrosity" of the masses that the scientific and artistic technicians of the culture were catering.[4]

Not everyone agreed, of course, that the situation was so dire. David Manning White, an early student of pop culture, for instance, offered a sharp critique of the doomsayers. In the middlebrow literary magazine *The Saturday Review*, White pointed out that the critics of mass culture seemed to assume that without the products of the new technology the cultural tastes of the masses would be much higher. In fact, he observed, "the critics who develop such a frenzy over the stereotyped activity of the Lone Ranger as he shoots a couple of bad hombres on a Sunday afternoon" might consider that in the simpler nineteenth century, one of the most popular diversions in London had been bear-baiting. Although "there can be no defense . . . for certain aspects of our mass culture which are banal, dehumanizing and downright ugly," those qualities could be found in the entertainments of any age. Television, White argued, offered some serious drama, while paperback books, another medium of mass culture, made inexpensive editions of classics available to wide audiences. More Americans attended classical music concerts in 1955 than attended major league baseball games. As for totalitarianism, Germans had more high culture than any nation in history when in 1932 they voted Hitler into power.[5]

The most vocal critics of mass culture would have none of this balance-sheet tallying of gains and losses from the new media. In their view, a cultural revolution had already taken place. "In none of the archeological ages," wrote Bernard Rosenberg, a New York intellectual associated with the magazine *Dissent*, "has human society been so revolutionary as in the present." For a million years humans had been forced to struggle for subsistence. Now, suddenly, with new technology that was spreading around the world, "the curse of Adam is being lifted" and "manual labor is becoming obsolete." At least the prospect was that masses of people were being freed from the "drudgery, monotony, inanition, and brutishness" of constant work for mere survival. "The precondition for transfiguring *Homo sapiens* into a higher species begins to exist," wrote Rosenberg. The tragedy was that "before man can transcend himself he is being dehumanized. . . . Freedom is placed before him and snatched away. The rich and varied life he might lead is standardized." Growing "more alike than ever" bred anxiety, loneliness, and a sense of loss of meaning: "And even if the incubus of hydrogen war could be lifted, these specters would still hover over us." Such a sense of emptiness could have disastrous political implications. "At its worst, mass culture threatens not merely to cretinize our taste, but to brutalize our sense while paving the way to totalitarianism," Rosenberg said. American freedom itself might be at stake.[6]

At an all-star conference on "Mass Culture and Mass Media," held in the fall of 1959, the leading expert on totalitarianism, Hannah Arendt, tended to side with such pessimists. One of the many impressive German Jewish émigrés who had become leaders among American intellectuals, Arendt was already famous for her 1951 book *The Origins of Totalitarianism*. She soon would be writing on Adolf Eichmann, a functionary in the Holocaust, and "the banality of evil," a phrase suggesting that degraded cultural sensibilities left people susceptible to totalitarian control. Although she was not as alarmist as Rosenberg was in seeing mass culture as the direct road to tyranny, she expressed concerns, like Macdonald's, that modernity was turning culture (in the sense of the arts) into objects of consumption. That meant that higher culture was inevitably being debased as its purveyors tried to turn it into something that would be more entertaining and hence more widely consumed. The assumption behind her analysis was that societies needed intellectual, artistic, and literary leadership. She did point out that there had never been a golden age of high culture led by intellectuals, especially not in America. Nonetheless, she agreed that the current "malaise of the intellectual" sprang from the fact that intellectuals found themselves surrounded by educated people who were rewriting, digesting, condensing, or adapting high culture to make it more consumable by the masses "to persuade them that *Hamlet* can be as entertaining as *My Fair Lady*, and educational as well." Consumerism had become a nearly all-controlling force in the modern era. Everything had come to be valued in terms of its function. What was being lost was the ability to love the world for its own sake, to value art simply for its beauty. "We can say without exaggeration," Arendt wrote, "that a society obsessed with consumption cannot at the same time be cultured or produce a culture."[7]

Novelist James Baldwin, speaking at the same conference, was just as pessimistic but much less inclined to blame the failing of mass culture on the banality of its producers. Instead, he was alarmed at the "overwhelming torpor and bewilderment of the people" who consumed it. "I am less appalled by the fact that *Gunsmoke* is produced than I am by the fact that so many people want to see it," Baldwin wrote. Both the producers of American culture and its consumers were "afflicted by the world's highest standard of living and what is probably the world's most bewilderingly empty way of life." In that setting, the role of the arts had become largely to shield people from these realities, since that was what they wanted. So, for instance, two recent "superior" movies, *The Bridge on the River Kwai* and *The Defiant Ones*, could not "really be called serious." *Kwai*—the heroic story of British prisoners of war sabotaging a Japanese bridge project—put the viewer at a safe remove from a "kind of madness . . . that is far more dangerous and widespread than the movie would have us believe." And the suggestion of *The Defiant Ones*—about two escaped prisoners (played by Sidney Poitier and Tony Curtis) chained together as they tried to elude their pursuers—that "negroes and whites can learn to love each other if they are only chained together long enough runs so madly counter to the facts that it must be dismissed as one of the latest and sickest of liberal fantasies." Americans, said Baldwin, had expectations that they could somehow be lifted above "the same catastrophes, vices, joys, and follies, which have baffled and afflicted mankind for ages." They did not want to admit that "the American way of life [had] failed—to make people happier or to make them better." They persisted in believing that social ills were the result of a handful of aberrants or of "some miscalculation in the formula (which can be corrected)." So the people wanted a popular art that shielded them from the perennial truths about "sad human nature."[8]

The most impressive voice at the conference for a more moderate view was that of Edward Shils, a highly regarded sociologist at the University of Chicago. In response to the thoroughgoing pessimists, Shils made the case that new mass culture and mass media were not necessarily destructive either of high culture or of the quality of civilization. Shils agreed with other analysts that a whole new order of society had taken shape in the United States and other leading industrialized nations just since World War II. But, unlike many other observers, Shils believed that this unprecedented "mass society" had many virtues. Its distinctive feature was that the new technology allowed all people—despite their differences in ethnicity, class, region, or religion—to be incorporated into the central institutions of the society, since they were more immediately connected with the center than the masses had been in earlier large-scale societies. This new order tended to diminish the sacredness of authority and the power of tradition. At the same time, such a society fostered a greater degree of civility than existed in the past societies. This civility was built upon a moral recognition of commonalities that came from living in the same human community. Certainly there was a long way to go, said Shils: hierarchical features, racism, and other prejudices persisted. "Nonetheless," he affirmed with a supreme confidence in the liberal hopes of the day, "the fact remains that modern mass society has reached out toward a moral consensus and a civil order congruous with the adult population." Rather than modern culture undermining higher values, "the sacredness that every man possesses by virtue of his membership in society finds a more far-reaching affirmation than ever before."

Contrary to pessimists such as Macdonald, Rosenberg, Arendt, or Baldwin, Shils believed that "mediocre culture" had many merits. "It often has elements of genuine conviviality, not subtle or profound perhaps, but genuine in the sense of being spontaneous and honest. It is often very good fun. Moreover, it is often earnestly, even if simply, moral." Even the vulgar and sometimes brutal lower mass culture—in sports, games, crude comedies, and popular songs and dances of the emerging youth culture—despite its impoverished symbolic content, was not all bad for introducing the masses into some sort of shared culture. Furthermore, although there may have been some decline in superior culture of late, there was no reason why superior culture could not flourish side by side with the inevitably larger mediocre culture and contribute to its improvement.

What is wrong, said Shils, "is wrong with the intellectuals and their institutions" and had little to do with culture produced for the mass media. American intellectuals tended to disdain every other elite in America and to disparage politics in such a way as to follow either of two courses: to come up with frivolous and now embarrassing Marxist solutions, as they so often did in the 1930s, or to simply fail to contribute anything to ameliorating the relationships among the various levels of culture. The sense of alienation among intellectuals was nothing new, and it was hardly constructive. True, some had become popularizers who had sold their souls. But the solution was for the best intellectuals and artists to simply do their jobs well, producing works that were truly great. If they did this, there would be "nothing to fear from the movement of culture in mass society."[9]

From the perspective of half a century later, a striking feature of these exchanges is the assumption that intellectuals and artists should provide cultural leadership for the society as a whole. As one of the conveners of the 1959 conference put it, all sides "tend to agree . . . that the health of mass culture is dependent on the vitality of elite culture."[10] The same might have been said of almost any such discussions of the topic throughout the decade. On the one hand, it might not seem surprising that a collection of academics, intellectuals, and writers would think that the future quality of civilization depended on people like themselves. But on the other hand, few such persons today would entertain similar illusions; they would simply assume that society was so fragmented that no one group, especially not a group of intellectual elites, could guide the whole.

One assumption of the midcentury era was that a society normally should have an overall cohesion. It would be shaped by a prevailing "climate of opinion" that ideally would be shared to some degree at all levels of society. Similarly, people often talked of "the American character" as though it were more or less one thing. Another assumption was that highly cultured men (including a few women) ought to be in some way guiding the society by providing its highest intellectual and artistic expressions. Most intellectuals and literary people were alarmed that higher culture was being overwhelmed by technologically driven mass culture and populist and business-class anti-intellectualism. But as Edward Shils argued, that alarm could be seen as an expression of the insecurities of the intellectual class, and even those anxieties suggested that the ideal of intellectual leadership, however beleaguered, still had some life.

One reason that the fulfillment of such aspirations appeared at least plausible in the relatively conservative 1950s was that the cutting-edge liberal intellectuals of that era typically viewed themselves as the true guardians of the Western heritage. That way of thinking is in marked contrast to the culture-wars model that emerged a generation later, in which leading intellectuals and academics often emphasized subversion of the inherited ideals of the "imperialist" West. It also stood in strong tension during the 1950s themselves with the avant garde visual artists of the day, who anticipated the fragmentation of the heritage. For the aspiring intellectual and literary leaders of that time period, the dangers seemed largely those that came from the barbarians from below and the economic, social, and political forces and ideologies that might exploit them. Both World War II and the Cold War were about saving whatever was moral and good about Western civilization from forces that might distort and obliterate that heritage. Those goods were expressed in the best and most humane ideals found in the great literature, philosophies, and even some religious classics of the heritage. That was the heart of the higher education that was to help rebuild civilization after the war. Few aspiring intellectual leaders questioned those humane ideals. The challenge was to sustain them in the United States, which was renowned for its anti-intellectualism.

American intellectuals of the 1950s accordingly spent a good deal of time worrying about their own status and whether it might be declining.[11] The McCarthyite efforts of the first half of the decade to root out Communists and former Communists from government and academia had a strong populist anti-intellectual component. The intellectuals had also regarded Adlai Stevenson as self-evidently the most thoughtful presidential candidate, and were chagrined when in 1952 and 1956 he was repudiated by the masses, in part for being regarded as too much of an "egghead." The members of the intelligentsia were not, however, ready to give up on democratic politics, as evidenced by their enthusiasm for the Harvard-educated John F. Kennedy in 1960. The deeper issue was whether intellectual leadership could be sustained in populist democratic America.

The ideal of a coherent society with intellectual leadership went back to the Greeks and the Romans, but it had been revived during the enlightenment of the eighteenth century.

The intervening era of church domination had provided a heritage of thinking of Christendom as a single entity united by a common faith. When Western Christendom fragmented after the Reformation, and neither Protestants nor Catholics could command the whole, the notion persisted that a basis for the cultural unity of Western civilization could be found— but now in some sort of universal reason. That ideal would place intellectuals in the forefront among the shapers of culture. In the nineteenth century, that concept found romantic expression in a movement that added artists and writers to the list of the bearers of the best in the culture, as expressed, for instance, in Ralph Waldo Emerson's depiction of a heroic and free "American Scholar." More influentially, the Marxist mix of romanticism and science had evolved into the Bolshevik belief that the "intelligentsia" could speak for the masses. American intellectuals, many of whom had at least flirted with such outlooks during the 1930s, retained the idea that they should be leaders who were shaping the culture as a whole. John Dewey, the most influential American philosopher and educator of the first half of the twentieth century, proposed "a common faith" based on secular principles.[12]

By the end of the 1950s, historian Richard Hofstadter was working on what would become his classic study of the threats to the ideal of intellectual leadership: his Pulitzer Prize–winning *Anti-intellectualism in American Life*, published in 1963. Hofstadter traced the historical roots of what he depicted as the ominous "anti-intellectualism in our time." He defined anti-intellectualism as "a resentment and suspicion of the life of the mind and of those who are considered to represent it."

Hofstadter cited Billy Graham as one of his exhibits of contemporary anti-intellectualism and gave primacy in his historical analysis to the revivalist tradition in religion and the fundamentalist "revolt against modernity."

In Hofstadter's jeremiad, there was a lost golden age, the enlightened era of the founders. (The irony of the contrast to the later populist appeals of the religious right to the "Christianity" of the founders is worth noting). "When the United States began its national existence," wrote Hofstadter, "the relationship between intellect and power was not a problem. The leaders *were* intellectuals." That era soon gave way to populist anti-intellectual counterforces, ending definitively with the 1828 defeat of John Quincy Adams ("who could write") by Andrew Jackson ("who could fight"). Hofstadter had already depicted, in his 1955 book *The Age of Reform*, the paranoid style of the populist politics of the late nineteenth century, which had anticipated elements of McCarthyism. In addition, Hofstadter believed, American business culture, faith in practicality generally, the popularity of self-help techniques, and the experience-over-content views of education had all contributed to the current sad state of American society. Hofstadter, as a historian, was quicker than most of his peers to see the roots of the mass society in earlier American experience, but these precedents provided all the more reason to fear that democracy based on intelligent regard for the best humanistic values of the civilization might be destroyed by the shallow fickleness of mass culture and mass man.[13]

The status anxieties of the midcentury intellectuals were possible only because they had what in retrospect looks like considerable status. There was still something of a national conversation on the state of civilization, and the intellectuals themselves had a prominent place in that conversation. Even looking back from a few decades later, the 1950s would look like a sort of golden age for American intellectuals.[14] An ideal was still intact—the notion that the culture of the nation might be guided by a broad inclusive national consensus—and academics and other intellectuals were more on the inside of that project than not. They recognized that their position was precarious, but they had reason to be hopeful that they could play major roles in guiding the national dialogue. In that respect they were heirs to a hope that had been strong among the educated in Western civilization since the eighteenth century: the hope that a humane, cultured elite might provide the society with direction and coherence.

TWO

Freedom in the Lonely Crowd

THE ANXIETIES OVER TELEVISION, MASS MEDIA, AND a culture dominated by mindless anti-intellectualism were all premised on that deeper concern that the world might be witnessing the emergence of a whole new creature, "mass man" or "modern man." Those were people whose lives were shaped not by traditional cultures but by the demands of ur- banized, industrialized, and commercialized modern life, of which shallow mass culture was one expression. The West had dominated much of the world for centuries, but some- thing essential about the heritage of Western civilization was possibly about to be lost. Since America was leading the way into modernity, that cultural erosion might be weakening the American moral character and the collective ability of Amer- icans to remain as a free people. As Bernard Rosenberg put it in an alarmist, but not unusual, form, "At its worst, mass culture threatens not merely to cretinize our taste, but to bru- talize our sense while paving the way to totalitarianism." At stake, then, in countering the modern trends that degraded the quality of human experience, might be nothing less than loss of freedom.[1]

"Freedom" was much celebrated in midcentury America and was a word one could use without explanation or argument. The massive sacrifices and destruction of World War II had been justified in the name of freedom. The Cold War was defined in the West as a struggle between Communist totalitarianism and "the Free World." But beyond simple political freedoms and not being taken over by foreign powers or by totalitarian dictators, what did "freedom" mean?

What is fascinating and revealing is how easily talk about the unassailable ideal of "freedom" in a political sense blended into an ideal of personal attitudes of independence from social authorities and restraints. A key word that was often used to express this taken-for-granted ideal was "autonomy." To be autonomous means literally to be a law unto oneself. In a more popular sense it meant simply to be a free, self-determining individual. It meant to "think for oneself," which was the highest ideal of education. The standard advice of graduation speeches was "just be yourself," or "be true to yourself." The opposite of autonomy was "conformity." Everyone, it seemed, agreed that one should not be a conformist.

We can get a sense of the times and of its characteristic perceptions of the forces shaping modern society by taking a brief excursion through some of the popular social analyses that dealt with the modern threats to freedom in the sense of personal autonomy. As one follows these accounts of the forces shaping individual lives in modern times, there are a number of questions to keep in mind. What were the assumptions underlying the analyses? What were assumptions, for example, regarding human fulfillment, and regarding the relationships of individuals to their societies and to subcommunities? What was the role of science in relation to other authorities? Was science an aid to freedom, or a threat to it? What sorts of forces or trends were popular writers and their readers noticing then that seldom draw comment today? What was taken for granted that might not be taken for granted today? Which of the characteristic ideals of that era are still very much alive and shaping contemporary culture?

The best-known work relating the rise of totalitarianism to wider issues of personal freedom in society was Erich Fromm's *Escape from Freedom*, first published in 1941 and still widely read in the 1950s (it went through three printings in 1959 and 1960 alone). Fromm was one of those remarkable Jewish émigrés who had become influential in almost every area of American thought and the arts. (One list includes forty-three such figures, from Albert Einstein in science to the composer Arnold Schoenberg.) As in the case of Hannah Arendt, the fact that he was a refugee from Hitler's Europe made his analysis of the rise of totalitarianism all the more compelling. Fromm was not a systematic historical thinker like Arendt, explaining totalitarianism in terms of multiple levels of causation. He was, rather, an engaging synthesizer, who sketched the big picture in broad and often speculative strokes and who offered engaging insights to which general audiences could easily relate.[2]

The problem, said Fromm, was with freedom itself, that most celebrated achievement of modernity. "Modern man,"

Fromm explained, had been freed from both the restraints and the securities of pre-individualistic societies, "but has not gained freedom in the positive sense of his intellectual, emotional and sensuous potentialities." Even though freedom "brought him independence and rationality," it also "made him isolated and thereby anxious and powerless." Rather than advancing to the realization of the true freedom "based upon the uniqueness and individuality of man," he had retreated into "new dependencies." Voluntary submission to totalitarianism was the most dramatic symptom of this regress. But Americans could also see it much closer to home in the conformity of modern society, in which "the individual ceases to be himself" and "adopts entirely the kind of personality offered by the cultural patterns," so that "he becomes exactly as all others are and as they expect him to be."[3]

Fromm was a master of the grand generalization in describing the evolution of modern culture and of modern man. Trained in sociology, he fashioned his historical interpretations with an air of scientific authority. The two great forces shaping the historical evolution of the collective attitudes of societies, he believed, were the economic and psychological factors. Fromm was most interested in the psychological ones. In the early modern era, Westerners believed that humans were essentially rational and driven by self-interest. Sigmund Freud exploded that view by showing that humans were most often driven by irrational and unconscious forces. Fromm saw himself as a follower of Freud, but he was also critical of the father of psychoanalysis, believing Freud was too rooted in his own time and place and not aware enough of how historical developments transformed societies and their collective psyches. Fromm nonetheless borrowed psychoanalytic categories for his explanations of historical developments. For instance, he attributed the rise of Hitler to the appeal of sadomasochism. Sadism was related to the inbuilt human will to power, and masochism reflected the tendency "*to get rid of the individual self, to lose oneself*" or "*to get rid of the burden of freedom.*" Or, in order to make clear he was not talking about just neurotics, regarding normal people this tendency could be described as simply the "*authoritarian character*" who "admires authority and tends to submit to it, but at the same time he wants to be an authority himself and have others submit to him."[4]

Fromm turned his analysis most directly on affluent America in 1955 in *The Sane Society*. In the modern world, he argued, even free societies could be insane, or organized on a pathological basis that undermined the fulfillment of truly humanistic values. At the end of the Middle Ages, "man discovered nature and the individual, . . . laid the foundations for the natural sciences and developed humanistic ideals that combined the moral conscience of the Judeo Christian tradition with the intellectual conscience from the Greek tradition." But, in recent centuries, technological and industrial gains, rather than advancing those ideals, had subverted them. "In building the new industrial machine," Fromm explained, "man became so absorbed in the new task that it became the paramount goal of his life." Human energies, "which once were devoted to the search for God and salvation, were now directed toward the domination of nature and ever-increasing material comfort." As mechanization dramatically advanced these material goals, "man himself became a part of the machine, rather than its master." Contemporary societies, whether totalitarian or capitalist, organized everything efficiently, and everyone was to fit in like "a cog in the machine." In such societies, Fromm wrote, "happiness becomes identical with consumption of newer and better commodities." But affluent Americans typically became quickly bored with their material things. So the rates of alcoholism and suicide in America were among the highest in the world, and escapist entertainments were everywhere. Modern societies promoted short-term "happiness," but they did not cultivate truly humanistic lives characterized by relatedness, creativity, individuality, loving relationships, reason, and "a frame of orientation and devotion."

The commoditization and objectification of modern capitalism thus produced, to use two of the most popular terms of the day, "alienation" and "conformity." The idea that capitalism led to the alienation of humans from their true selves went back to Karl Marx, but Fromm argued that Marx entirely missed the irrational side of humans. Furthermore, contrary to Marx, Fromm said that in highly industrialized societies alienation was rampant regardless of who controlled the means of production. In America, the widely noted conformity illustrated how widespread alienation was in a consumerist society. In the Soviet Union, conformity might be imposed from above, but in the United States it was voluntary. Vast numbers of Americans chose to eat tasteless and non-nourishing white bread and to drink Coca-Cola because these products were the most effectively advertised and marketed. The new suburbs, with rows of similar houses, likewise illustrated the leveling of tastes. The new suburbanites typically said they did not want to "stick out" too much. Conformity to whatever one's neighbors did was the new authority. Psychological problems had become matters of "adjustment" to conventional norms.

Fromm, ever the optimist about human potentialities, did not think it was too late to change. Declaring that time was short, he concluded with a sermonic peroration: "We are in reach of achieving a state of humanity which corresponds to the vision of our great teachers; yet we are in danger of the destruction of all civilization, or of robotization. A small tribe was told thousands of years ago: 'I put before you life and death, blessing and curse—and you chose life.' This is our choice too."[5]

Fromm appealed to American audiences in part because he was a moralist who adopted the classic American sermonic form of the jeremiad, a lament for a lost golden age.[6] Fromm identified the Renaissance as this ideal time, a time when Judeo-Christian moral consciousness combined with Greek respect for intellect and when modern science was emerging. Although he criticized the thinkers of the eighteenth-century enlightenment as having too naïvely trusted in reason and for neglecting the irrational, he nonetheless shared with them the confidence that, with proper scientific analysis of the human condition, it should be possible to construct an enlightened society in which peace, brotherhood, and cooperation would prevail.

More immediately, Fromm's ideas resonated with the mainstream American conversation of the mid-1950s because he provided an engaging diagnosis of a malady that one of his former students, David Riesman, had already named in the title of his famous 1950 book *The Lonely Crowd*. Riesman wrote as an academic sociologist, and not in as accessible a style as Fromm's, but, like his former teacher, he offered to the general reader a wide-ranging historical and contemporary analysis framed into a few easy-to-remember categories. Despite the academic character of the work, his categories caught on, and by 1954 Riesman had reached what at the time was the closest thing to canonization in America by appearing on the cover of *Time*. As one commentator remarked at the end of the decade, "*The Lonely Crowd* is like a lot of books that have permanently changed men's minds": far more people knew its thesis or had looked into it than had actually read it.[7]

Why did the basic motifs of Riesman's rather turgid analysis resonate so well with middlebrow audiences? The answer is that he was addressing, with a scientific aura, one of the most compelling questions regarding the human condition, a question that had already attracted the interest of many thoughtful people. The question was whether the typical "modern man" had become alienated, inauthentic, conformist, and phony. Every educated person would have been familiar with the theme, as it had appeared in recent popular works of literature. Arthur Miller's long-running 1949 play *Death of a Salesman* was among the most prominent of these. Willie Loman, the salesman dominated by his hopes for economic success and being "well liked," became a symbol of the emptiness of modern times. Countless other literary and artistic works, both at home and abroad, presented complementary themes. One could reflect on the emptiness of modern life in Jean-Paul Sartre's *No Exit*, for example, where hell is to get what one always wanted in life: to be regarded in the perception of others. Or, in Albert Camus's *The Stranger*, one might contemplate the meaninglessness of modern existence. Ralph Ellison's *The Invisible Man* in 1952 offered an African American depiction of the artificiality and alienation in the modern world. For middle-class college students who were fretting about becoming conformists, no text was more canonical than J. D. Salinger's 1951 book *The Catcher in the Rye*, with its depiction of the phoniness of adult life. No longer was it easy to believe, as it had been in the 1930s, that politics and ideologies might offer real answers. Just as the title of the 1955 novel and 1956 film *The Man in the Gray Flannel Suit* became another catchphrase to summarize the problem, so the title of the immensely popular 1955 James Dean film *Rebel Without a Cause* came to encapsulate the worry that there might not be a solution.[8]

Riesman addressed these same sorts of issues, but with a weight of scientific authority that offered historical perspective. He divided all societies into three broad types: "tradition-directed," "inner-directed," and "other-directed." These categories, which he recognized were "ideal types" that glossed over many exceptions, had to do with how each of these sorts of societies most typically shaped the "mode of conformity" or "social character" of its members. Most societies throughout history, including Europe in the Middle Ages, had been "tradition-directed." In such societies, people typically inherited a fixed status, and their lives were shaped by rituals, routines, and religious beliefs and practices that carried the divine authority of countless ages. Societies in the second category, the "inner-directed" ones, were in transition, notably Europe since the Renaissance and the Reformation. In these societies, economic expansion brought an ever-increasing number of choices and an ever-greater degree of personal mobility. Although there were many varieties of inner-directed people, they typically *internalized* the traditional and religious ideals and goals of their societies, so that they were guided by a sort of internal moral compass. The Protestant work ethic, which contributed to the rise of capitalism, would be a classic example of the internalization of religiously sanctioned ideals and the extension of them to new settings. Hard work and self-denial were characteristic of successful individuals in such societies when the societies were shaped by expanding industrial production. Inner direction, according to Riesman, had dominated the early modern era and the beginning of the twentieth century, and most Americans had been brought up with something like that ideal.

In the past few decades, said Riesman, a new type, the "other-directed" person, was emerging, especially among the younger and more well-to-do people in the more progressive urban and suburban population centers. This new middle class, although not yet in the majority, was likely to soon be the most common American type. The distinguishing characteristic shared by other-directed people was that their goals and values were shaped by their contemporaries, either known to them directly or indirectly through the mass media. Their mode of conformity was to internalize perceived current opinion and make it their own. In that respect they resembled the small groups of elites in cultures of the past for whom fashion served as a substitute for custom and morals.

These types of societies reared their children in different ways. Whereas inner-directed child rearing was directed toward teaching virtues, disciplines, and standards that would build character, other-directed child rearing was more permissive and oriented toward forming the personality. As other-directed children grew up, they would be able to adjust readily to ever-changing fashions and to present themselves as an attractive product by current standards. Often, those standards were shaped by advertisers' representations of the advantages of what were in fact marginal features of their products. The inner-directed schoolroom might be decorated with pictures of the ruins of Pompeii, or a bust of Caesar, objects that "signal the irrelevance of the school to the emotional problems of the child." The other-directed school would be much more oriented toward cultivating the personal development of each child. The walls would be decorated with the children's own artwork, which was part of a program of "the socialization of taste." Changes such as these signaled a broader cultural change "from morality to morale."

The ideal that Riesman took for granted as the antidote to modern conformity was "autonomy." To be autonomous meant to be an authentic, self-determining, and self-fulfilled person who could transcend the conventions of one's society. Yet, he was vague as to how that goal was to be accomplished. In his preface to the 1960 edition of *The Lonely Crowd*, Riesman explained that he was not writing out of nostalgia for a past when inner-directedness was the rule; nor was he equating inner-directedness with autonomy or even arguing that it was necessarily superior to other-directedness. In fact, he did not think that any individual person entirely fit these ideal types. People could achieve autonomy within either framework, particularly if they understood the forces that were shaping them. Social science, then, could be liberating, as it might help people identify the social roots of their problems. But finding a solution that would be consistent with the ideals of self-determination and autonomy seemed to be up to them. Riesman made a point of counting lack of dogmatism as among the virtues of his outlook. "*The Lonely Crowd,*" he wrote in 1960, "was one of a number of books which in recent years have eschewed dogmatism and fanaticism and preferred openness, pluralism, and empiricism." Here was another set of words—"openness, pluralism, and empiricism"—that could be taken for granted as representing ideals shared by those who were forward looking. They were ideals that would help ensure autonomy for scientific researchers and other thinkers.[9]

IN THE LATE 1950S, the danger of losing autonomy to the subtle forces of a capitalist society was a hot topic. The subject inspired a series of best-sellers, beginning with William Whyte's *The Organization Man*, which became a "must read" in 1957. Whyte was a journalist who wrote for *Fortune*, a business magazine. He claimed that he was not writing about "mass man"; or attacking TV sets, ranch wagons, or "gray flannel suits"; or even making a plea for "nonconformity." Yet his book seemed to be an extended riff on David Riesman's other-directed man as found among corporate executives and aspiring executives. These "organization men," Whyte argued, were molded by an "ideology" of the corporation. ("Ideology" in this era was almost always a bad thing.) These were men "who have left home, spiritually as well as physically, to take the vows of organization life." They were uprooted and transient in that they would give up all other connections to move whenever the corporation demanded it. They were thus, like priests, part of a collective, and they had internalized the corporation's "social ethic," or "a body of thought that makes morally legitimate the pressures of society against the individual." This ethic included three fundamental propositions: "a belief in the group as the source of creativity; a belief in 'belongingness' as the ultimate need of the individual; and a belief in the application of science to achieve the belongingness."

Whyte differed from Riesman in one important respect. Whereas Riesman believed that social scientific understandings of the human condition would be liberating, Whyte regarded "scientism" as one source of the problem. Scientism was helping to destroy America's vaunted tradition of rugged individualism. Ever since Isaac Newton, Whyte observed, people had been claiming that if scientific methods could control nature, they ought to be able to resolve human problems as well. Whyte quoted a typical statement made at a gathering of social scientists: "More than ever, the world's greatest need is a science of human relationships and an art of human engineering based on the laws of such science." Often, proponents of such views would observe that if only the money spent on the atom bomb had been spent on human science, the world would be a far better place. Believers in scientism, said Whyte, were happy that modern ethical relativism had removed narrow traditional restraints on human behavior. Social scientists often invoked an ideal for society as though they were medical doctors restoring "equilibrium," or bringing about "adjustment" in place of conflict and maladjustment. "There is not one section of American life," Whyte warned, "that has not drunk deeply of the promise of scientism." Its ideals were in the schools, in aptitude tests, in mass communications, and elsewhere, and surely there were few who had not had "a personal collision with it."

Scientism had made inroads into the social fabric because it characteristically appeared only as part of a larger social ethic that presented itself as beneficent. That ethic was especially explicit in the giant corporations that stressed the values of togetherness and belongingness. It was an ethic that declared that individuals found their meaning in groups that worked together and socialized together. Whyte illustrated these ideals extensively in corporate life. He also described the social structures of the new model suburbs, such as Park Forest, Illinois, or Levittown, Pennsylvania. In the suburbs, uprooted people learned to value the more extroverted parts of their personalities as they sought togetherness in community activities and places of worship. Their greatest desire for their children's education was that they would learn social skills. America, said Whyte, was cultivating "a generation of technicians" who would be skilled psychologically "to cope with the intricacies of vast organizations." These "technicians" had learned to accept and understand their roles as the "interchangeables" of corporate society. They were, as they said, "all in the same boat." But, Whyte added, "where is the boat going? No one seems to have the faintest idea; nor, for that matter, do they see much point in even raising the question."

Whyte offered little by way of solution. The forces that were swallowing up the individual were probably not inexorable, he thought. Western society needed to reassert the ideal that had animated it since the end of the Middle Ages, "that the individual rather than society must be the paramount end." It was essential for individuals who were caught in the corporate web to resist the ideology. "Any real change will be up to the individual himself," Whyte wrote. People needed education and perspective to recognize the problem. But, other than that, all Whyte had to suggest in his closing paragraph was that, "He must *fight* The Organization." Here was autonomy again. The fight would not be crude or in the streets, but from within. The ideology would constantly be asking the individual to surrender to the idea that there was no conflict between the individual and society, but the individual must never believe that. The only answer, then, seemed to be an affirmation of the heroic individual who was willing to be true to himself. In other words, it was all right to dress in a gray flannel suit and drive your station wagon to the suburbs, so long as you had the heart of Thoreau.[10]

Whyte's appeal is as revealing of the times as are his arguments. He oversimplified the trends that he documented, and oversimplifications are the stuff of best-sellers. But for understanding the era, one may ask why these particular oversimplifications would hold such attraction for readers. The popularity of *The Organization Man* suggests that many

Americans who were thoughtful enough to buy this lengthy study (471 pages) were ready to believe that the forces of regimentation in their society were creating a version of Brave New World that was so subtle that the intricacies of its science-driven, soul-destroying tendencies needed to be exposed. A decade later, the children of the suburbs would be taking a similar message to the streets. But even at the height of the 1950s, the unnerving sense that something was going dreadfully wrong in technological civilization was already there, even among the people who read *Fortune* magazine.

BY THE SECOND HALF OF 1957, another national alarm was sounding about the subtle loss of freedom. This time it was in sociologist Vance Packard's *The Hidden Persuaders*, which held the number-one nonfiction best-seller slot. (The fiction best-seller during this time was *Peyton Place*, which provided a very different version of the theme that America was not all it seemed on the surface.) The threat from advertising, Packard emphasized, was even greater than most people realized. Packard warned that people should be especially alarmed about how advertising agencies were increasingly using motivational research. Products were not being sold on their merits, but on the basis of researchers' calculations of people's most characteristic irrational needs and desires. The marketers were controlling people's choices through effective image making. In the "disturbing Orwellian configurations of the world through which the persuaders are nudging us," people were losing their freedom to make rational decisions.[11]

The larger force destroying freedom, as Packard elaborated in two sequels, *The Status Seekers* of 1959 and *The Waste Makers* of 1961, was consumerism. In a time of unprecedented abundance, powerful economic interests were dedicated to maximizing consumption. These interests were armed with technical expertise directed toward manipulating almost every aspect of American life. As Packard summarized the threat at the end of *The Status Seekers* (which also was a number-one best-seller): "The forces of the times seem to be squeezing individuality and spontaneity from us." Drawing on a motif of the end-of-decade anxieties over possible lost American ideals (as in "Our National Purpose" or "Have We Gone Soft?"), Packard affirmed that "we profess to be guided in our attitudes by the body of ideals set forth by our Founding Fathers. The Founding Fathers would wish us to be individualists, free thinkers, independent in mind and spirit."[12]

By the end of the decade, warnings against conformity had become standard American wisdom. A typical example was a 1958 *Reader's Digest* article, originally from *Woman's Day*, on "The Danger of Being Too Well-Adjusted." The article pointed out that great men often were not well adjusted, so women should be flexible in their expectations for their children. The author quoted a psychologist who claimed "we've made conformity into a religion." The psychologist assured mothers that each child was different "and ought to be." Notably, *Woman's Day* was not applying the lesson to the roles of women themselves.[13]

Of all the popular analyses of "modern man," however, a late entry, Betty Friedan's 1963 book *The Feminine Mystique*,

"Just once I'd like to pick up a woman's magazine that doesn't tell you how to make your husband happy."

Mischa Richter, June 14, 1958, *The New Yorker*

proved to have by far the most traceable impact in fostering social change. One of the great unspoken assumptions of the social discourse of midcentury America, an assumption intertwined with the enlightenment trust in rationality and the individual, was that the discourse was essentially about males. Friedan herself used the term "modern man," but when she used it, the great difference was that she insisted on the genuinely inclusive sense of the term. So when Friedan, like the other analysts, examined self-realization versus self-alienating conformity, she applied the diagnosis to the other half of the "modern" population that was invisible in most of the other analyses.[14]

Like many of the other social commentators, Friedan was alarmed by the conformity and uniformity of the suburbs, but in her case the concern arose from her own experience. Betty Goldstein (her maiden name) had been an honors graduate from Smith College in 1942. During and after the war, she had lived in Greenwich Village and worked as a reporter for a labor magazine. She married Carl Friedan in 1947, and after her pregnancy with their second child was forced to give up her job. She and Carl, a theater producer, moved to various suburbs, where she raised a family and attempted to do a little reporting on the side. Her illumination came in 1957, when she was asked by the women's magazine *McCall's* to write an article on the fifteenth anniversary of her Smith graduating class. She found that many of her classmates shared her frustrations with raising children in the suburbs and living in the shadow of their husbands' more exciting worlds. She also found the members of the class of 1957 to be passive and conformist. So instead of writing the article on the "togetherness" of women that *McCall's* wanted, she issued a sharp call for liberation that none of the women's magazines would publish. She did find an editor at Norton who liked her idea as a book, however, and after five years of research and writing she finished her game-changing task.[15]

Since Friedan's point of reference was her own experience as a college-educated woman living in the suburbs, when she spoke of modern "man," she, like the other analysts, was not thinking of a wide and diverse range of American men and women, but rather of the "modern" middle-class person of the cities and suburbs. Friedan was distressed mainly by the psychological implications of the mystique that insisted that educated women were best fulfilled by living through their husbands and children. She saw this ideology of domesticity as having been greatly revived just after World War II. After a famous chapter in which she compared the way in which the "women who live in the image of the feminine mystique trapped themselves within the narrow walls of their homes" to the way in which prisoners learned to "adjust" to concentration camps, Friedan turned to the alternative. All sorts of scientists of human behavior, she pointed out, had been moving toward a consensus that a basic human need was to grow. It was "man's will to be all that is in him to be." Her list included Fromm and Riesman, and also a dozen other leaders in psychology, such as Abraham Maslow, Carl Rogers, Gordon Allport, Karen Horney, and Rollo May. Each of these, she said, as well as theologians such as Paul Tillich and many existential philosophers, agreed on the need for the organism to grow to self-realization, or "will to power," "self-assertion," dominance," or "autonomy."

Friedan recognized better than some of the social scientists that this ideal was not so much established by scientific research as it was the postulate on which some promising research was based. But she did take as accepted science "the fact that there is an evolutionary scale or hierarchy of needs in man (and thus in woman), ranging from the needs usually called instincts because they are shared with animals, to needs that come later in human development." Women were being blocked from the highest sort of personal growth and development. "Despite the glorification of 'Occupation housewife,'" Friedan declared, "if that occupation does not demand, or permit, realization of woman's full abilities, it cannot provide adequate self-esteem, much less pave the way to a higher level of self-realization." In one of the few studies in which these sorts of categories had even been applied to women, Abraham Maslow had confirmed that what he called "the high-dominance woman," or one who was more akin to men in her attitudes, "was more psychologically free—more autonomous." By contrast, "the low-dominance woman was not free to be herself, she was other-directed." High-dominance women, said Maslow, were even better fulfilled sexually than low-dominance women. Riesman had observed that men in mass society needed meaningful work; just the same, said Friedan, applied to women. Enlisting the term that just recently had come into vogue, housewives had lost touch with their true selves and were suffering from an "identity crisis."[16]

Friedan was writing on the eve of America's greatest national identity crisis since the American Revolution itself, and the parallel between the individual and national challenges can be instructive. If many individual American women and men were suffering from identity crises in the 1960s, they could, as Friedan was pointing out, at least turn to a consensus extending from theologians to scientists to pop culture that they should be pursing an ideal of freedom and self-fulfillment.

Aside from its later impact on the women's movement, what were the practical implications of this ideal of freedom in the sense of personal autonomy for ordinary Americans?

It is, of course, impossible to measure that in most cases. Perhaps the most practical impact would be the message it sent to young people growing up in any one of the countless American subcommunities. If one were a young person growing up in a Polish Catholic neighborhood in Chicago, in a Jewish community in Brooklyn, or in a small town of the Midwest or the South, the implication of the message was that one should get out from under the petty constraints of local communities and traditions and be true to oneself. One then needed also to avoid the conformity and alienation in the marketplace or the suburbs—something that might prove more difficult.

The problem was that freedom is often largely a negative term: "just another word for nothing left to lose," as Janis Joplin would famously sing shortly before her death in 1970.[17] So if one sought to construct a new identity, the ideal of autonomy did not in itself provide a standard for determining what constituted self-fulfillment. Once one was free from restrictive traditions or expectations, what was going to replace them as a basis for determining what was good for human flourishing? The critics of modernity were warning that one must be vigilant against the demands of hyperorganized commercial society and consumerism lest they undermine one's true humanity. Yet, it was not clear what criteria one should use to determine what the positive alternatives were to the shackles either of traditionalism or of modern conformity.

THREE

Enlightenment's End?
Building Without Foundations

THE SOCIAL COMMENTATORS WHO IDENTIFIED CONFORMITY as a preeminent modern problem could assume that autonomy was the solution because they were taking for granted that there were better values that authentic, self-fulfilled people could draw upon. John Dewey, the highly influential philosopher and educator, for instance, had proposed in the 1930s that "a common faith" could be built around self-evident "goods of human association, or arts, and of knowledge." Dewey presented these ideas as self-evident principles. "We need no external criterion and guarantee for their goodness," he affirmed. "They are had, they exist as good, and out of them we frame our ideal ends." Dewey's liberal heirs in the 1950s spoke much the same way, as though there were such common "goods," which autonomous persons of goodwill could recognize and around which a healthy society might be built.[1]

One can better understand the basis for such confidence among the centrist liberal proponents of this outlook by looking at how they defended it—not against opponents, but against those whom they regarded as heretics. A heretic is not the advocate of an entirely opposing ideology, after all, but an insider, someone who believes that he or she is speaking for the tradition but has come to conclusions that others in the community denounce as unorthodox.

In this case, the heretic was one of the most distinguished sages of the time, Walter Lippmann. His heresy was to say that his liberal colleagues were trying to build a public consensus based on inherited principles, even after they had dynamited the foundations on which those principles had first been established. The result was that liberal culture, of which he was a part, had no adequate shared criteria for determining "the good." Lippmann's proposed solution seemed to his peers to be much better fitted to the eighteenth century than to advanced twentieth-century thought. The story of what proved to be Lippmann's last book, *Essays in the Public Philosophy*, published in 1955—and the negative reactions of his fellow liberals to that book—highlights one of the great unresolved issues of the day.[2]

At midcentury, Lippmann had just turned sixty, and he was unquestionably a leading figure in shaping the American liberal consensus. A renowned journalist and author, he was the prototype of the public intellectual. He had grown up in a well-to-do Jewish family, had been educated at Harvard, and had become one of the first Jews to be fully accepted into the cosmopolitan mainstream. While still in his mid-twenties, in 1914, he had helped to found *The New Republic*, and he had already published the first two of what would become a score of influential books. His best-selling 1929 book *A Preface to Morals* was perhaps the volume that best stated the problems inherent in the transition America was undergoing at the time—the transition from the moral confidence of the Progressive era to the uncertainties of postwar modernity. Lippmann's fame and influence continued unabated into the era of the Cold War—in fact, he was the one who had popularized the term "Cold War," in a 1947 book title. His writings, including countless editorials, were unquestionably among the leading works of the day, setting the agenda for discussions of American democratic civilization and its future.[3]

Lippmann signaled by his title, *Essays in the Public Philosophy*, that he would be addressing one of the most important questions of the time: On what philosophical basis might America build a unified public culture, given all its diversity? He began his answer in a prophetic mode, titling his opening section "The Decline of the West," and recounting the essential twentieth-century political problems that he had been writing about for four decades. From his point of view as "a liberal democrat," the crucial question of the age was whether "both liberty and democracy can be preserved before the one destroys the other." The danger was that democratic government would be overwhelmed by mass opinion, which had proved itself incapable of responding rationally to society's rapidly changing needs. Lippmann had already written on this topic eloquently and influentially in the 1920s, and Hitler's popular support in his rise to power in the 1930s had proven that his fears were more than justified. "The impulse to escape from freedom, which Erich Fromm has described so well," Lippmann wrote, confirmed the broader urgency of addressing the underlying issue.

That deeper issue was the vogue of moral relativism. Specifically, Lippmann was concerned that there were no longer any transcendent moral standards to which to appeal in guiding either the government or the people. In the first half of the twentieth century, there had been a trend to separate the law from reference to any higher moral system. Lippmann had now come to see that as a dangerous innovation. The institutions of free societies, he observed, had been founded "on the postulate that there was a universal order on which all reasonable men were agreed." In the era of America's founding, even if the more secular thinkers and the traditional Christians may have differed on the exact source of that order and its content, "they did agree that there was a valid law which, whether it was the commandment of God or the reason of things, was transcendent." Speaking of such essential principles as "freedom of religion and of thought and of speech," Lippmann affirmed that "the men of the seventeenth and eighteenth century who established these great salutatory rules would certainly have denied that a community could do without a general public philosophy." But the idea, so essential to establishing democratic institutions, that there was such a higher moral order had not survived modern pluralism, and "with the disappearance of the public philosophy—and of a consensus on the first and last things—there was opened up a great vacuum in the public mind, yawning to be filled."

The task of building consensus and community, as Lippmann saw it, was not just a matter of forging agreements on policies here and there; ultimately, it would rest on underlying philosophical and moral assumptions. One of the effects of pluralism was that morality had come to be thought of as an essentially subjective and private matter. "It became the rule that ideas and principles are private—with only subjective relevance and significance," he wrote. Lippmann saw that same trend in philosophy. Referring to Jean-Paul Sartre's existentialism, Lippmann declared that "if what is good, what is right, what is true, is only what the individual 'chooses' to 'invent', then we are outside the traditions of civility." With no objective point of moral reference, with no philosopher to teach people that there was any order or meaning beyond the subjective self, there was nothing with which to counter the madness of the masses or to preempt their madness by educating them in the traditions of civility.

The only hope for reestablishing a public philosophy, and thus for preserving free institutions, said Lippmann, was a recovery of natural law. He asserted this point not so much as a philosophical argument as a philosophical agenda. He did not define natural law beyond referencing an article on it by Mortimer Adler, a Jewish scholar who had long been its chief secular advocate. Nor did Lippmann say precisely how natural law was to be discovered. Rather, by a recovery of "natural law," he meant a return to the conviction that had long been basic to Western thought: that there was some sort of objective moral order or set of timeless moral principles that could be discovered through rational inquiry. The common law and the principles of a free society, he believed, could be sustained only on such a basis. "Except on the premises of this philosophy," he declared, "it is impossible to reach intelligible and workable conceptions of popular election, majority rule, representative assemblies, free speech, loyalty, property, corporations and voluntary associates."[4]

Walter Lippmann was, as one of his closest friends said of him, very much "a child of the enlightenment,"[5] and it is helpful to think of him and his project as a public intellectual in that framework. As a quintessential cosmopolitan without strong connections to any ethnic or religious community, he was deeply committed to a universal order of civility. That commitment was in harmony with the outlooks of many of the nation's eighteenth-century philosopher-founders, such as Franklin, Jefferson, and Madison, who wanted to get away from the authority of sectarian subcommunities and to build a larger order on self-evident principles on which people of goodwill ought to agree. In the Progressive era of the early twentieth century, such cosmopolitan outlooks fit the agenda of many of America's leading thinkers who were trying to establish common principles for public life that would transcend local and parochial prejudices. Lippmann studied at Harvard with the famed philosophers William James and George Santayana, and he had been very much in sympathy with the early twentieth-century challenge of how to reconstruct a public philosophy that would meet the demands of the modern age.

The great modern intellectual challenge to establishing a universal philosophy was Darwinism. Prior to Charles Darwin, it had been difficult even for the more secularly minded to imagine a universe that was not the product of an intelligence. Hence, it had seemed likely that humans should be able to discover some transcendent moral order. Darwin made it plausible to imagine that both the universe and humans themselves were the products of chance natural forces. In that case, moral systems were all human inventions and were best understood by their comparative histories. Added to these theoretical issues was the practical matter that the United States, by the beginning of the twentieth century, was becoming increasingly diverse. How could one reconstruct a common philosophy in such a world?

Walter Lippmann's teacher William James offered constructive principles that might point to a way out. According to James's pragmatism, we can find out which beliefs to hold on to as "true" by seeing which ones prove themselves most effective in getting us into adjustment with the rest of our experiences with reality, including the beliefs we already firmly hold. That is to say, in effect, that rather than descending into relativism or skepticism, we could rely on a sort of survival of the fittest of beliefs, some of which we could accept as true because they have proven to work in the real world.[6]

Early in his career, Walter Lippmann adopted an outlook that had a Jamesean hue. "We have to act on what we believe, on half-knowledge, illusion and error," he wrote in 1913 in his first major book, *A Preface to Politics*. "Experience itself will reveal our mistakes," he continued. "Research and criticism may convert them into wisdom." He also, as was common in the Progressive era, had faith that the scientific method could bring people of diverse interests into practical agreement. "The discipline of science," he wrote in *Drift and Mastery* in 1914, "is the only one that gives any assurance that from the same

set of facts men will come approximately to the same conclusion." Science was the best hope humanity had in the face of
modern pluralism. "And as the modern world can be civilized
only by the effort of innumerable people," Lippmann declared,
"we have a right to call science the discipline of democracy."[7]

By the time Lippmann published *A Preface to Morals* in
1929, the confidence of the Western world in scientifically
based mastery of human problems had been badly shaken by
the disaster of the Great War. The 1920s had become the era
of "the disillusion of the intellectuals." As Lippmann put it, the
present was "the first age . . . in the history of mankind when
the circumstances of life have conspired with the intellectual
habits of the time to render any fixed and authoritative belief
incredible to large masses of men."

Lippmann went on to argue, in contrast to the moralistic
platitudes of Protestant theological modernists, that it was time
to face frankly the irreversible reality of this breakdown of the
old authorities and to reconstruct humanism on a new, secular
basis. The fundamental problem for the modern moralist, he
declared, "is how mankind, deprived of the great fictions, is to
come to terms with the needs which created those fictions." Still
reflecting the spirit of William James, Lippmann was proposing
that the constructive moralist should look beneath the varieties
of formal systems for the insights into human experience that
have been discovered and rediscovered through the ages.[8]

Despite the enthusiastic reception of *A Preface to Morals*,
by the early 1930s the combination of increasingly skeptical
intellectual trends, the Great Depression, and the spread of totalitarianism had made such gentlemanly constructive prag-

matism problematic. In 1929, the same year that *A Preface to Morals* appeared, journalist Joseph Wood Krutch published *The Modern Temper*, in which he argued that evolutionary naturalism, if consistently applied, undermined not only traditional religion but also traditional moralities. Supposed moral norms were, after all, nothing more than survival mechanisms from more primitive times. Evolutionary naturalism, he emphasized, had the necessary implication of undermining all moral authority. Carl Becker, a leading historian of the era, argued for a skeptical pragmatism that anticipated later twentieth-century views regarding moral systems as simply the useful constructions of those who were in power. In his classic 1932 book *The Heavenly City of the Eighteenth Century Philosophers*, Becker maintained that the enlightenment thinkers were really men of faith as much as men of reason. They had an unfounded faith that the universe was the product of a deity and that there were objective natural and moral laws that reason could discover. Their outlook, Becker argued, was thus closer to that of the medieval thinkers of the thirteenth century than it was to that of truly modern thinkers who realized they lived in a chance universe.[9]

LIPPMANN DID NOT SHARE such radical skepticism, but by the mid-1930s he was wondering about the ability of modern liberal culture and modern science to find an adequate basis for building a moral community. The darkening clouds of totalitarianism as well as the deep economic depression made it a real question as to whether democracies could survive. Lippmann at first supported the New Deal, but he then became dubious of the government's ability to solve societal problems through pragmatic and increasingly collectivist action. It was around this time, in the later 1930s, that he began to take up the project that would eventually become *Essays in the Public Philosophy*. Lippmann had begun to question the conclusion of his liberal contemporaries that modern natural science dictated a rejection of eighteenth-century views of natural law, especially of a higher moral law, as irrecoverable mythology. Lippmann had begun to think, rather, that twentieth-century mainstream Western thought had taken a serious wrong turn into a dead end. Pragmatism by itself could not get them out. Therefore, it was time to see if somehow a higher moral law might be recovered as a basis for a shared social morality.[10]

Lippmann's proposal was complicated by the fact that, by the 1950s, natural-law philosophy was chiefly associated with Roman Catholicism. Anti-Catholicism was still strong in much of American life. Since the 1930s, many liberals, including both mainstream Protestant and secular liberals, had associated Catholicism with fascism. After World War II, it had been commonplace to ask whether Catholicism was compatible with democracy. When in 1949 journalist Paul Blanshard argued in *American Freedom and Catholic Power* that true freedom and true Catholicism were incompatible, his book reached the best-seller lists. In 1951, William F. Buckley, a Roman Catholic and a recent Yale grad, created a furor in his *God and Man at Yale* by alleging that education at Yale was relativistic and atheistic. The anti-Christian stance of many of the faculty, he said, was of a piece with their being on the wrong side of the battle between individualism and collectivism. In

1955 Buckley founded *The National Review*, a crucial step in launching a new conservatism. At the time, however, the fact that Senator Joseph McCarthy, whom Buckley supported, was a Roman Catholic heightened liberal fears that Catholicism might be associated with repression.[11]

So when Lippmann's *Essays in the Public Philosophy* appeared in 1955, his call for a return to natural law was weighted with so much cultural baggage that it easily triggered alarms disproportionate to what he had actually said. Even though he attempted to address the issues in the light of the long sweep of Western history, in 1955 the horizons of most liberal Americans were dominated by very recent memories of McCarthyism that were still smolderingly hot. Lippmann had opposed McCarthy, and he always thought of himself as a political liberal and a champion of free society, but to his great chagrin, a number of his mainstream contemporaries saw his ideas as a step toward authoritarianism. It did not help that he advocated, as a counter to enthusiasms of the masses, not only a rational search for natural law, but also a stronger executive. *The New Republic* characterized his book as the work of a "badly frightened man." *The Saturday Review* called it "eloquent but unconvincing." Reinhold Niebuhr acknowledged Lippmann's "profundity" but did not have much else good to say. Not all the reviews were negative, but the gist of most of them was, as *The Nation* put it, that it was "not the great book of distilled wisdom on the ultimate problems of political organization and human destiny for which we have been waiting."[12]

The most scathing attack came from Archibald MacLeish. The poet, who also had been Librarian of Congress during the

FDR administration, had come under some fire himself from McCarthy because of some minor left-wing associations. In a long review, he took Lippmann to task for not sufficiently countering McCarthyite threats to basic freedoms. Lippmann, said MacLeish, was motivated by "the conviction that the idea of full individual freedom and the idea of effective community are irreconcilable ideas and that there is therefore an ineluctable choice between them; that in that choice community must be preferred." According to MacLeish, Lippmann had mistaken the direction of history. "The flow of human life is not backward toward closer and closer association but forward toward greater individuality." MacLeish believed that artists were on the cutting edge that pointed to the direction in which civilization was headed. "In all the modern arts of words, in modern painting, in modern music, a common impulse is at work," he wrote, "an impulse, almost a compulsion, to penetrate the undiscovered country of the individual human consciousness, the human self." Lippmann, by contrast, by stepping away from the priority of freedom and looking toward the past, was playing into the hands of McCarthyites and other authoritarians.[13]

Lippmann offered a rejoinder in which he could barely contain his anger that MacLeish had accused him of somehow abetting McCarthyism. MacLeish had opened with a lengthy exposition of the implications of the McCarthyite menace, and only when he was well into his polemic did he get around to mentioning that Lippmann had a long record as an editorialist of speaking out forcefully against McCarthyism. Lippmann retorted that he would have to have a personality as split as that

"*It's true, sir, that the State Department let me go, but that was solely because of incompetence.*"

Alan Dunn, June 17, 1950, *The New Yorker*

of Jekyll and Hyde to truly have advocated such opposites. He was just as much a genuine liberal and a champion of the free society as he had ever been. MacLeish, he continued, had confused categories regarding human freedom. MacLeish had declared that since the eighteenth century, Americans had been committed to "the boundless liberty of the *individual human spirit.*" But then MacLeish had equated that with "the modern democratic belief in the greatest *possible* individual freedom." Lippmann could affirm the ideal of "the boundless liberty of the *individual human spirit*" as an ideal truly for the individual. But in the *public* sphere it was not "possible" that freedom could be boundless for everyone. The best we could do would be to work for the greatest freedom possible *within the bounds necessary for community*. Freedom in the public domain, said

Lippmann, must necessarily be limited (even while it should be maximized). MacLeish had defined "the basic philosophy of liberalism" as "the belief in the liberation of the individual human spirit to find its own way to enlightenment and truth." With this Lippmann could agree. But that ideal for inward individual self-fulfillment was hardly a complete standard for a *public* philosophy that would adjudicate the hard questions that arise when individual interests conflict.[14]

In *Walter Lippmann and His Times*, a tribute from a dozen of the leading thinkers of the day published in 1959 for Lippmann's seventieth birthday, Arthur Schlesinger Jr. offered a piercing analysis of what, from a liberal perspective, was Lippmann's fall not only from pragmatism, but also from pluralism. In his books of the 1920s, said Schlesinger, Lippmann had addressed the irreducible pluralism of modern societies with a procedural solution of "the maintenance of a regime of rule, contract, and custom." But since then, and especially in *Essays in the Public Philosophy*, these practical rules had somehow taken on a sort of cosmic essence for Lippmann. Due process had grown into "a universal order on which all reasonable men were agreed." These rules were to be objectively discovered and had to be obeyed. Rather than seeing pluralism as a reason to back away from absolute claims, Lippmann had declared that "in this pluralized and fragmenting society a public philosophy with common and binding principles was more necessary than it had ever been." Moreover, Lippmann had insisted that the truths of such a philosophy would have to be such that they could be "proved to the modern skeptic" so that "only the willfully irrational can deny" them. Schlesinger did not think himself irrational, "yet for those brought up in the tradition of James, Lippmann's conception of natural law, for all its nobility, cannot help seem an artificial construct." Schlesinger even asked, with a mix of hope and condescension, whether, in some of Lippmann's very recent statements, there were "perhaps signs that he is swinging back to a more vivid appreciation of the reality of pluralism?"[15]

Schlesinger represented the antidogmatic liberal consensus of the era as well as anyone. He had, in fact, been one of the first to define it in his 1949 book, *The Vital Center: The Politics of Freedom*. Liberals of his generation (he was born in 1917), he explained, had not grown up with the romanticism of utopian Marxism that had captured the hearts of so many progressives, but rather, with the ugly realities of the Soviet Union and the hopeful experimental politics of FDR's New Deal. Influenced by theologian Reinhold Niebuhr (Schlesinger became a prime example of "atheists for Niebuhr"), he affirmed that radical reformers had naïvely optimistic views of human nature and hence of its reformability. Democracy supported a healthy balance between individual fulfillment and community responsibility and was "a process, not a conclusion." It needed to be characterized by "empiricism and gradualism." Such centrist liberal views, built around "the spirit of human decency," said Schlesinger, could in fact be characterized as a "new radicalism" opposing the extremes of tyranny. It "dedicates itself to problems as they come, attacking them in terms which best advance the human and libertarian values, which best secure the freedom and fulfillment of the individual."[16]

Sociologist Daniel Bell encapsulated much the same out-look in the much-noted title to his 1960 book of essays, *The End of Ideology*. Marxism was no longer an option for intel-lectuals, but that was only a symptom of a larger phenome-non, that all ideologies were exhausted. Analysts needed to give up searching for global schemes and recognize that re-ality was too complicated for that, and so needed to be stud-ied one problem at a time. What was needed, Bell counseled, was the scholar rather than the intellectual. "The scholar has a bounded field of knowledge, a tradition, and seeks to find his place in it, adding to the accumulated, tested knowledge of the past, as a mosaic." The scholar's work was much more down to earth and empirical than the intellectual's. And the practical, down-to-earth challenge for Western society was the same as it had had been for "the last two hundred years: how, within the framework of freedom, to increase the living standards of the majority of people and at the same time maintain or raise cultural levels."[17]

Scholarly public intellectuals such as Schlesinger and Bell were not rebels without a cause, but moderate reformers with many causes. They articulated the widely held view that the strength of the American democratic system lay in the very feature that worried Lippmann, its relativism and lack of dogmatism. Dogmatic ideologies had been the bane of the twentieth century. Forward-minded American thinkers could look to the New Deal as providing a refreshing contrast that they saw as capturing the genius of the American way. Arthur Schlesinger Jr., who bridged the two eras by being both the preeminent historian of the New Deal and a special adviser to

President Kennedy, described the ideal. "The whole point of the New Deal," he wrote, "lay in its belief in activism, its faith in gradualness, its rejection of catastrophism, its indifference to ideology, its conviction that a managed and modified capitalist order achieved by piecemeal experiment could combine personal freedom and economic growth." Daniel Bell, in an introduction to a 1955 volume analyzing McCarthyism and the new American right, found similar traits throughout American history. Americans, he observed, long had been given to extremism in morality, but they had seldom extended such moral dogmatism to politics, where instead they displayed "an extraordinary talent for compromise." That talent for "bargaining and consensus" grew out of "the historical contribution of liberalism," which was "to separate law from morality."[18]

Yet the fact was that, despite such disclaimers, the champions of a pragmatically based consensus were themselves moralists. They were passionately committed to principles such as individual freedom, free speech, human decency, justice, civil rights, community responsibilities, equality before the law, due process, balance of powers, economic opportunity, and so forth. And they were morally indignant at those who might subvert those principles. Yet their justification for these principles was not that they were fixed in a higher law or derived from an ideology. Rather, it was that these principles had evolved historically in the give and take of human experience in free societies and had proven themselves as contributing to human fulfillment. Mainstream liberal thinkers could thus, on the one hand, be consistent believers in a purely naturalistic universe that did not furnish any absolute first principles, yet on the other hand have a dedicated faith in the shared principles of the current American consensus. They were, as one commentator characterized them, "believing skeptics."[19]

In retrospect, the striking thing to notice about mainstream liberals' faith is that they believed that their pragmatically based relativistic democratic principles might lead to a pluralistic or inclusive mainstream cultural consensus that, at least ideally, might be resisted only by reactionaries and ideologues on the fringes. By the end of the 1960s, any such hopes, even as just an ideal, had proven fanciful. Rather than America being an ever-broadening consensus society, drawing peoples of all ethnicities, races, and religions into the mainstream, it became glaringly apparent that the nation was made up of many subcommunities and interest groups, and that, despite many shared beliefs, some of their fundamental principles were incompatible with those of others. Young and old, white and black, pacifist and patriot, religious and secular, liberal religious and conservative religious, women and men, gay and straight, were all contending with each other, and there was no single set of principles by which to adjudicate the differences.

How was it possible for so many liberal thinkers of the midcentury to retain their faith in what amounted to the enlightenment conclusions of the founders ("liberty and justice for all," and the like) while dismissing the enlightenment foundations on which those conclusions rested? Why did they not, like Lippmann or conservative thinkers of the day, see that the edifice on which they were building their pluralistic consensus was about to collapse? How could they be both skeptics regarding fixed first principles *and* believers in the principles of the American way?

The answer is that at the time the outlook seemed to make good sense as a comparative matter. Compared to the alternatives, especially compared to the incredible brutalities of twentieth-century totalitarianism, the prevailing American principles had indeed proved themselves. Unprecedented prosperity, moreover, had validated that the American capitalist system, for all its faults and inequalities, worked; it was even subject to incremental improvements. World War II had generated patriotism, loyalty to the American way, and dedication to freedom, and these shared ideals persisted in the Cold War. Furthermore, if one accepted the premise that natural scientific assumptions and methods provided the closest thing to objectivity that could be obtained, and the corollary that no religious or metaphysical creed could plausibly claim universality, then the nondogmatic relativistic pragmatic method of testing beliefs seemed the best hope for building a unified society.

In an era when World War II and the Cold War had created an unusual sense of unity, it seemed plausible not to worry about first principles. As Yale political scientist Robert Dahl put it in his 1956 book *A Preface to Democratic Theory*, "the assumptions that made the idea of natural rights intellectually defensible have tended to dissolve in modern times." Still, that was no great concern, because the "strange hybrid" of the American political system had proven remarkably adaptable in its evolution over time. Or, as Dahl's Harvard counterpart, Louis Hartz, put it: "We have made the Enlightenment work in spite of itself, and surely it is time we ceased to be frightened of the mechanisms we have derived to do so."[20]

At a time when such was the standard wisdom, Walter Lippmann appeared rather old-fashioned, at least when in the company of other liberals, in seeing the lack of foundations as so fundamental a problem as to demand a collective rebuilding of philosophical first principles. In many respects, the enlightenment still reigned in America, yet it continued to reign only by default. Lippmann's disagreement with his peers was not over whether a unifying consensus based on the founders' enlightenment principles should continue—they all agreed on that—but over whether it *could* long endure without the foundations on which the founders had built.

Such debates regarding pragmatism versus natural law might seem abstract and theoretical, but their implications were no better illustrated than in the greatest domestic political struggle of the late 1950s and early 1960s: the civil rights movement.

Looking back from the twenty-first century, it is easy to see that there was a lot missing from the inclusive pluralism of the midcentury public intellectuals. The insiders were almost all white males; most were secularists; some had a Protestant background, but more were Jewish; and almost all lived in the Northeast. Catholics were useful because of their urban political power, but they were only barely beginning to gain a voice in national discussions and were not a discernible presence in major universities. Fundamentalists and evangelical Protestants were off the radar of most academics and cultural observers, except as reminders of anti-intellectualism in the nation's hinterlands. Those observers also regarded the South as largely a cultural backwater. Ethnic Protestants, even some with considerable intellectual traditions, received no more hearing than ethnic Catholics. Hispanic and Asian Americans likewise were not thought of except as among those who would be drawn into the consensus.

African Americans, however, were a glaring absence. Unlike most other outsiders, they were not only largely ignored, they were often excluded, and that exclusion permeated almost every dimension of their lives. Many liberal intellectuals accordingly recognized racial discrimination and lack of "Negro" civil rights as the most flagrant reproach to American democracy. Arthur Schlesinger Jr., for instance, in his 1949 manifesto *The Vital Center*, declared that "the sin of racial pride still represents the most basic challenge to the American conscience," and that even though we cannot "transform folkways and eradicate bigotry overnight," we must "maintain an unrelenting attack on all forms of racial discrimination."[21]

With the 1954 US Supreme Court decision mandating school integration, and President Eisenhower's use of federal troops to enforce integration in Little Rock, Arkansas, in 1957, everyone had to include racial issues as being among the top challenges facing the nation. Where one stood on the question of how fast the nation should move on the question of civil rights was a pretty good index of the degree of one's liberalism. In an era when liberals, with their emphasis on incremental changes, often looked like conservatives on many social issues, ending racial injustice was a matter on which they were typically dedicated to advocating substantial social change.[22]

Despite such dedication, one great shortcoming of the approach of consensus liberals to civil rights was that they, like the federal government itself, had no real solution to the problem of southern white intransigence. In general, the liberal political establishment held a view of human nature that was too naïvely optimistic to overcome the entrenched power and deeply held racial prejudices that undergirded southern public segregation. Arthur Schlesinger Jr., who may be taken as prototypical of the most thoughtful of such centrist liberals, partook in this naïveté. Despite being an admirer of Reinhold Niebuhr, Schlesinger did not take to heart the degrees to which human perversity could disrupt the operations of the pragmatic vital center. Thus, Schlesinger was so confident in the incremental problem-solving approach of the American experience that he could declare, "I am certain that history has equipped modern liberalism . . . to construct a society where men will be both free and happy." His hope, which was typical of the liberalism of the time, was that prejudice would eventually yield to education. Already in 1949 he could claim with ungrounded optimism that "the South on the whole accepts the objectives of the civil rights program as legitimate, even though it may have serious and intelligible reservations about timing and methods."[23]

In fact, efforts at incremental change only increased the backlash among southern white racists, and it took the African American protest movement to turn the tide. Martin Luther King Jr.'s effective leadership in that movement was built around a combination of the fervor of southern black revivalism and the power of nonviolent resistance. What might not be quite as evident is that the doctrine of nonviolent resistance was based on a realistic view of human nature that power must be met with power. King recognized that a people without political power could nonetheless mobilize their moral power if they were willing to suffer in the cause of justice. To get that to happen, he drew on a tradition of fervor in the black churches.[24]

It needs to be added that, underlying these essential factors, what gave such widely compelling force to King's leadership and oratory was his bedrock conviction that moral law was built into the universe. In this he was different from most of the liberal proponents of civil rights. His conviction was grounded in his Christian beliefs, which in turn were shaped by the "personalist" theology he had studied at Boston University. Personalism was an idealist philosophy based on the premise that God's person was the center and the source of reality, and hence that human personality had moral significance in that it participated in that most basic aspect of reality. King said that personalism helped him to sustain a faith in a personal God. Integral to that faith was the conviction that God had "placed within the very structure of the universe certain absolute moral laws."[25]

Everything else that King advocated for the movement followed from this confidence in a moral order. King believed that God was working in history toward bringing justice and his kingdom, although the process was not direct or inevitable, but involved human agency in combating evil. The power of nonresistance was a moral power that was built around the belief that all people have some degree of moral sensibility, and so moral suasion is a real form of power. Further, central to all moral actions must be the recognition that all persons, even one's enemies, are of infinite worth, because they are created in the image of God. Since personality is at the center of reality, history cannot be explained simply by economic forces, but is more basically a matter of personal and moral relationships. The goal of society, King proclaimed, ought to be a "beloved community" in which "brotherhood is a reality." King blended his progressive idealism with the American political heritage ("let freedom ring") in such a way as to revive the founding ideals with a latter-day force.[26]

Appeal to a higher moral law was the centerpiece of King's 1963 "Letter from the Birmingham Jail," in which he admonished moderate white clergy for thinking it "unwise and untimely" to resist unjust laws. For such an audience King invoked St. Augustine to argue that "an unjust law is no law at all," and St. Thomas Aquinas to say that "an unjust law is a human law that is not rooted in eternal and natural law." King elaborated his personalist test for what was rooted in eternal or natural law: "Any law that uplifts human personality is just. Any law that degrades human personality is unjust." By that standard, "all segregation laws are unjust because segregation distorts the soul and damages the personality."[27]

King's invocation of objective moral law casts light upon the era in a couple of revealing ironies. Progressive observers celebrated King's stance and agreed that the segregation laws of the American South were self-evidently unjust. Yet the whole structure of King's thought and the motivation for his action rested on theistic and higher-law premises that many of those same observers believed to be self-evidently untrue. Secular liberal pragmatists could share in King's moral indignation even while they lacked his rationale for universalizing such moral claims.

The other irony is that, just as the ideals of universal justice, equality, mutuality, peace, and integrated brotherhood were burning the brightest, they were lighting the torches of identity politics. By the time of King's death in 1968, the ideal of one American, integrated, consensus-based community had already flamed out, even though not everyone was ready to recognize that. Frustrated hopes had already turned portions of the African American community to Black Power and Black Pride. The African American civil rights movement became in some respects a model for other rights movements— particularly women's rights, gay rights, and rights for other minorities—but, although some of the rhetoric of justice and equality was similar, it was now reshaped by the frameworks of identity politics. Whatever the merits of these causes, rather than grounding reforms in a universalized moral order, their outlooks were often frankly shaped on perceptions and experiences unique to their group. American founding ideals, such as those of the self-evidence of rights to freedom and equality, were still often proclaimed as though they were moral absolutes, but they glittered as fragments in the ruins of the dream of shaping a nation on the basis of a universal moral order.

FOUR

The Problem of Authority: The Two Masters

IF NATURAL LAW COULD NOT BE REVIVED AS A SHARED basis for mainstream moral authority, where might such authority come from? There were, of course, shared American traditions, such as liberty and justice, national loyalty, and equal opportunity, that carried some presumptive weight. But by what standards was one to determine the meanings of these very broad concepts when they conflicted or were matters of dispute? Or, when it came to what might be taught in the universities, or in the public schools, or in the magazines, advice books, or guides to life, what were the most commonly shared cultural authorities?

At all these levels of mainstream American life, from the highest intellectual forums to the most practical everyday advice columns, two such authorities were almost universally celebrated: the authority of the scientific method and the authority of the autonomous individual. If you were in a public setting in the 1950s, two of the things that you might say on which you would likely get the widest possible assent were, one, that one ought to be scientific, and two, that one ought to be true to oneself. But despite the immense acclaim for each of these ideals, there was also a lurking question as to whether these two great authorities, the one objective and the other subjective, were really compatible with each other. The grand hope in the Western world in the eighteenth century was that they would be—that enlightened science would establish principles of individual freedom. But since then, from the romanticism of the nineteenth century through the scientifically augmented totalitarianism of the twentieth, there were many reasons to suppose that they might be in conflict. Such debates were still going on in the mid-twentieth century. Yet, despite such arguments, when it came to the practical aspects of life, the most common and influential cultural attitude was that science and freedom were complementary rather than contradictory.

As one might expect, the points of tension were most sharply defined in the highly intellectual field of philosophy. On the side of freedom and the individual was the vogue of existentialism in midcentury American thought. Existentialism was largely imported from continental Europe, and it had the appeal of offering a frank look at the human predicament. In the late 1950s and early 1960s, existentialism was popular among sophisticated college students, beatniks, and others looking for alternatives to American conformity, complacency, and scientism.

One can quickly gain an appreciation for the appeal of existentialism as an expression of dissent from the mainstream by looking at what became the canonical American summation of the outlook, William Barrett's 1958 volume *Irrational Man*. Barrett, a professor of philosophy at New York University, summarized existentialism and its critique of Western civilization's dependence on rationality with compelling clarity.

It took the disasters of the twentieth century, Barrett observed, for modern Europeans to recognize that the rational ordering of society and hopes for material progress "had rested, like everything human, upon a void." The modern person became a stranger to himself: "He saw that his rational and enlightened philosophy could no longer console him with the assurance that it satisfactorily answered the question What is man?" At the heart of existentialism, which Barrett illustrated in the philosophies of Søren Kierkegaard, Friedrich Nietzsche, Martin Heidegger, and Jean-Paul Sartre, was the project of facing the stark reality of one's own finitude, "the impotence of reason when confronted with the depths of existence, the threat of Nothingness and the solitary and unsheltered condition of the individual before this threat." The emphasis on human finitude had the appeal of countering the "can do" optimism about human abilities so common in most homegrown American outlooks.

Barrett characterized existentialism as "the counter-Enlightenment come at last to philosophical expression," saying that "it demonstrates that the ideology of the enlightenment is thin, abstract, and therefore dangerous." The rationality and technological reasoning of the modern post-enlightenment world had not freed people, but detached them from meaningful identities. The "lonely crowd" had been discovered by Kierkegaard long before it was documented by David Riesman. Contrary to the enlightenment, which put the essence of man in his rationality, existentialism dealt with "the whole man," including such "unpleasant things as death, anxiety, guilt, fear, and trembling, and despair." Modern man had tried to deny these realities or to explain them away through psychoanalysis. "We are still so rooted in the enlightenment—or *up*rooted in it—that these unpleasant aspects of life are like the Furies for us: hostile forces from which we would escape." The lesson of the twentieth century was that even "the rationalism of the enlightenment will have to recognize that at the very heart of its light is also darkness."

Despite this realism regarding the human condition, Barrett's existentialist solution otherwise fit much of the spirit of the time in emphasizing the primacy of the self. The difference from easy American optimism was, as he put it, "if, as the Existentialists hold, an authentic life is not handed to us on a platter, but involves our own act of self-determination (self-finitization) within our time and place, then we have got to know and face up to that time, both in its threats and its promises."

Existentialism represented one pole of philosophy and of midcentury culture and the arts—the pole celebrating individual freedom, self-determination, and even irrationality. Almost all of the rest of professional American philosophy clustered around the other pole, which flew the flag of rationality based on the scientific ideal. William Barrett was especially scathing in characterizing such tendencies among his fellow philosophers. In fact, if one wanted guidance regarding the meaning of life, he suggested, one of the least likely places to find it would be among professional philosophers. The dominant philosophies in American university philosophy departments, he observed, were examples of what had gone wrong in modern intellectual life. "The modern university," Barrett declared, "is as much an expression of the specialization of the age as is the modern factory." Modern knowledge had advanced through scientific specialization. Specialists focused on increasingly narrow and technical issues that only other specialists could understand. Philosophers, believing they needed to carve out a place for themselves in this scheme of things, had imitated the scientists in such specialization. Unlike physicists, however, whose retreat into esoteric specialization could eventually result in something as earthshaking as the production of the bomb, "the philosopher has no such explosive effect upon the life of his time." Rather, philosophers had given up any traditional role of being the sages who helped guide society and instead were finding that they had less and less influence on anyone beyond other philosophers. "Their disputes have become disputes among themselves," wrote Barrett.[1]

Barrett's complaint was based on the reality that American professional philosophy had come to be dominated by technical analytic philosophy, which indeed illustrated the disconnect between scientific models for knowledge and humanistic goals. These "logical positivists" were attempting to find definitive criteria for all genuine knowledge by carefully analyzing the differences between the language of hard empirical science and the less precise language used regarding ethics, art, or religion. The project of strict language analysis was developed by Bertrand Russell and G. E. Moore at Oxford University and in the early work of Russell's most brilliant student, Ludwig Wittgenstein, in the early 1920s. One can gain a sense of what was involved by looking at a relatively accessible encapsulation in A. J. Ayer's *Language, Truth, and Logic*. First published in Great Britain in 1936, Ayer's overview was still widely used as a text in American colleges in the 1950s.[2]

According to Ayer, philosophy was a specialized branch of knowledge that was distinguishable from natural science in that it dealt not with empirical verification, but with the logic of propositions that might be proven true. For statements to be true, they needed to be able to meet one of two criteria: either they were statements that were tautologies, or they were statements that could be empirically verified. If nontautological statements were not, at least in principle, subject to empirical verification, they were, strictly speaking, meaningless. With this breathtaking victory by definition, Ayer could sweep away centuries of metaphysical discussions as "superstitions" and dismiss the possibility that theological statements could make truth claims about God. For instance, a seemingly empirical claim of a personal encounter with a deity told us only about the mental state of the observer; it said nothing about the existence of a transcendent being, because it was a statement that had "no literal significance." Even an ethical statement, such as, "You acted wrongly in stealing that money," was a "pseudo-concept" with no factual content, and nothing more than an "emotive" expression of a moral sentiment. Logical positivists were not saying that theological, or ethical, or aesthetic state-

ments were pure gibberish and needed to be entirely abandoned. They were claiming these were just not the sorts of
statements that could be used to make true-false claims.[3]

By the postwar era, many of the analytic philosophers, most
notably Wittgenstein himself, were repudiating the strictest
early logical-positivist criteria as too rigid and as leading to a
sort of self-inflicted *reductio ad absurdum*. Nonetheless, logical positivism had helped to set the agenda of professional
philosophy as a narrow specialization dealing with language
and logic. Its purpose was to determine the most reliable foundations for a science of knowledge on which other sciences
ought to be built. This project has since come to be called
"classical foundationalism" by its many critics.[4] In terms of a
wider cultural analysis, one can see the dominance of analytical philosophy in American and British academia as a notable
instance of that side of modern culture that was attempting
to preserve the enlightenment ideal, an ideal that focused on
developing principles and procedures of rationality that ought
to command the assent of all open-minded hearers. Logical
positivism preserved that ideal of finding common ground,
but also pointed to the problem involved: strictly speaking (as
analytical philosophers were), such agreement could only be
established by severely limiting the range of rational discourse,
so much so that there was almost nothing left worth talking
about. No wonder, as William Barrett pointed out, that professional philosophy was one of the last places to go if one were
searching for the meaning of life.

Furthermore, as Barrett also observed, the differentia-
tion and specialization of modern intellectual life meant that

philosophers were not providing foundations for any thought beyond their own discipline. An intelligent generalist, such as Walter Lippmann—or any middlebrow person, for that matter—was not likely to find much guidance from academic philosophers. That was in marked contrast to the situation a generation earlier, when Lippmann had been able to bring the insights of his teacher William James into the public arena. Furthermore, not only did social philosophers not turn to the analytic philosophers for guidance, but also, and more ironically, neither did the practitioners of the sciences themselves. Natural scientists already knew what worked. Moreover, in the social sciences, specialization meant that each discipline was a sovereign domain in which practitioners set their own standards for how best to study the slice of human activity that their specialties considered.

Though not many people were saying it at the time, it was symptomatic of the crisis in the mainstream thought of the day that few people were listening to its most brilliant philosophers. Existentialists did offer insights on personal authenticity, but their following was small. Analytic philosophers searched for scientific-style verification, but they spoke almost only to each other.

If one is looking for the practical philosophies of the day that helped to shape the lives of ordinary people, the place to turn is the field of psychology. There one can find similar tensions between science and the individual, but in far more influential form. As psychology was a science, and one of its principal subjects was individual experience, it was inevitable that it would be a focal point for debates on the pivotal question of the day: How do scientific understandings of human behavior fit with faith in human autonomy and freedom? Western culture had inherited these two grand ideals, but did they support each other? In an era when many people had turned to psychology as a guide to life, that was a practical problem as well.

Although midcentury psychological theories related science to individual autonomy in many different ways, there were two views on the subject that marked opposite ends of the spectrum. These were the views represented first and foremost by B. F. Skinner and Carl Rogers.

B. F. Skinner is especially important to this issue because he was one of the few midcentury practitioners of the social sciences to directly address the question of the relationship between science and individual freedom. Skinner, born in 1904, grew up in a town in central Pennsylvania where he had from an early age challenged conventional authorities, and he was always an independent thinker. In addition to being trained as an experimental behavioral psychologist, he was an inventor in the tradition of American tinkerers. In October 1945, *Ladies' Home Journal* featured his "baby tender," a climate-controlled box that he constructed for his own daughter to sleep in. His aim was to provide a safe environment for her that would also eliminate some of the burdens of parenting.[5] In experimental psychology his most important invention was the "Skinner Box," which was a mechanical device for automatically providing rewards to animals in order to reinforce their behavior as they were learning a task. Skinner was devoted to the stimulus-response model for understanding all learning, and he believed that the factors shaping human behavior and those shaping animal behavior differed only in complexity, not kind. People adopted behaviors that were positively reinforced, and they learned to avoid behaviors that were associated with unpleasant consequences or were negatively reinforced. As could be demonstrated with white rats in a Skinner Box, positive reinforcement worked better than punishments.

Skinner, although a critic of traditional faiths, was a true believer himself. With an unshakeable trust in the natural scientific method as the savior of humanity, he projected his mechanistic stimulus-response methodology into an entire philosophy of human nature. He first became well known for his utopian novel *Walden Two*, published in 1948. The book, which described a model community shaped by behaviorist learning principles, was in one sense a bold challenge to the temper of the times. Totalitarianism was an ominous threat, and Aldous Huxley's 1932 novel *Brave New World* had already become a canonical warning against mind control. Skinner nevertheless insisted that through the benevolent use of modern principles for controlling human behavior, people could be taught to live in idyllic harmony. From a consistently scientific viewpoint, he was fond of pointing out, each action or belief, including acts of will, must be determined by its antecedents. So the only real question, he argued, was whether we would continue to allow these external controls of human behavior to be accidental and haphazard, or should use our best knowledge to steer the controls in benevolent directions.[6]

Though Skinner always had many critics, his immense faith in the benefits of mechanistic science fit well with aspects of the temper of the postwar era. For most Americans, one of the most conspicuous dimensions of the times was the degree to which technology might make life easier and more comfortable. Many people remembered the time before they had automobiles, electric lights, radios, moving pictures, and indoor plumbing. Television and air conditioning promised new revolutions. Modern medicine and understandings of nutrition had made incredible strides since the late nineteenth century, so that people were living longer and growing taller. Modern science had defeated many ancient diseases, and "miracle drugs" brought amazing new triumphs. At the same time, there was no denying that modern science and technology had an equally ominous side. Not only had science been horribly misused in totalitarian states as an excuse for genocide, but the bomb made it all too likely that humans might blow themselves off the face of the earth.

Skinner acknowledged precisely these problems in his 1953 manifesto, *Science and Human Behavior*. "Man's power appears to have increased out of all proportion to his wisdom," he conceded. Man had "never been in a better position to build a healthy, happy, and productive world; yet things have perhaps never seemed so black." Nevertheless, it would be a great mistake, he argued, to blame science for these human failings. It was not the scientific method that was at fault, only its applications. "The methods of science have been enormously successful wherever they have been tried," he declared. "Let us apply them to human affairs." Most importantly, science should be applied to understanding human nature. "If we can observe human behavior carefully from an objective point of view," Skinner proclaimed with the self-confidence of an evangelist, "we may be able to adopt a more sensible course of action."

Skinner noted that many people resisted rigorous scientific objectivity in learning how to better control human behavior because they believed in a traditional concept of a free will that somehow "has the power of interfering with causal relationships and which makes the prediction and control of behavior impossible." Yet many of these same people also accepted that much of human behavior, including the will, was controlled by the external environment. They accepted that common people might hold backward views, or engage in superstitious practices, because of impoverished social environments. Or they recognized that the behavior of primitive peoples was shaped by their cultures. They might also acknowledge that children reared in Muslim countries were likely to become Muslim, and that those reared in Christian countries were likely to become Christian. Yet they did not recognize that faith might be based on an accident of birth. More broadly, they believed that elite people such as themselves transcended the social and cultural factors that shaped them. Skinner concluded that civilization was in a transitional stage in which many people clung to a doctrine of a mystical will that controlled itself, even while they acknowledged that some of the most highly regarded aspects of human behavior were shaped by cultures and by psychological antecedents. Recognizing that all behavior had causes was the first step toward learning to control and re-shape human activity for the better. So he affirmed, as though it were a grand millennial hope, that "it is possible that science has come to the rescue and that order will eventually be achieved in the field of human affairs."

As to the objection that human behavior and its causes might be so extraordinarily complex as to make prediction and control impossible, Skinner simply pointed out that scientists were only at the beginning of their quest to attain a systematic understanding of human nature and behavior. All that was needed was sufficient sustained attention to the problem. Science had come to understand much of what had formerly been thought of as being impossibly complex subjects. "Certainly no one is prepared to say now what a science of behavior can or cannot accomplish eventually," he affirmed. People had repeatedly underestimated what science could eventually accomplish.

According to Skinner, one of the things slowing down the progress of the science of human behavior was that people who could benevolently control others sometimes refused to do so. "The best example of this," said Skinner, "comes from psychotherapy," specifically from the views of Carl Rogers. Skinner quoted Rogers as saying basically that the therapist ought not to presume to control the client, because the client already has the means of control within. But whatever inner resources and inner will the person had, Skinner argued, had themselves already been controlled by external factors such as culture, ethical or religious training, education, government, and economic reinforcements, for good or for ill. So, in Skinner's view, counselors who had the knowledge and ability to provide some additional external control for the good would be shirking their responsibilities if they allowed patients to continue to be shaped by a host of capricious and unguided external controls.[7]

Carl Rogers's views, including his belief that scientific understandings could enhance genuine individual freedom, were far more typical of mainstream American attitudes of the time than were Skinner's. Rogers, born in 1902, had grown up in a strongly religious household in the Chicago suburbs; he had even studied for the ministry until he came to doubt his faith. By the World War II era, his work in what he came to call "client-centered therapy" had gained him a position at the University of Chicago. After the war he became the leading figure in the field as he caught the wave of the postwar popularity of psychological counseling and advice. "Professional interest in psychotherapy," he noted in the opening sentence of his influential *Client-Centered Therapy* in 1951, "is in all likelihood the most rapidly growing area in the social sciences today." He himself pointed out that his technique of nondirective counseling reflected the American spirit of the times. Freudianism, which became widely popular in America in the 1920s, emphasized the dark interior side of humans as defensive, self-interested creatures who were often shaped by the influences of unconscious and mysterious repressed desires. Rogers's client-centered approach, with its emphasis on bringing out the individual's innate power to work toward self-actualization and growth, resonated with prevailing American optimism regarding human nature and the celebration of freedom as a preeminent value.[8]

Rogers emphasized that client-centered therapy was thoroughly scientific. It had, he said, grown out of American psychology, "with its genius for operational definitions, for objective measurement, its insistence upon scientific method and the necessity of submitting all hypotheses to a process of objective verification or disproof." Hence, the hypotheses on which nondirective counseling were based "are testable, are capable of disproof, and hence offer a hope of progress, rather than the stagnation of dogma." So it was that psychotherapy was being "brought out of the realm of the mystical, the intuitive, the personal, the indefinable, into the full light of objective scrutiny."[9]

Skinner and Rogers thus became the prominent proponents of two sharply contrasting views of the implications of a scientific worldview for understanding human nature. Perhaps it was inevitable that they would clash, and indeed they eventually did. Rogers and Skinner aired their differences in a dialogue published in *Science* magazine in 1956. For his part, Rogers emphasized his agreement with Skinner that modern science could predict and control many aspects of human behavior. But the real issue, he said, was that of how human behavior should be controlled. Should the controls be consciously exercised from the outside, or should the goal be to develop "internal control"? Especially in the light of recent totalitarianism, Rogers believed, Skinner underestimated an important problem: that people corrupted by power might misuse external controls for evil purposes.

Although Rogers expressed unwavering faith in a scientific understanding of humans, he argued that natural science always takes place in the subjective context of the goals that science is to serve. "This subjective value choice which brings the scientific endeavor into being must always lie outside of that endeavor and can never become part of the science involved in the endeavor." Even as Rogers acknowledged that science could, of course, aid in refining the values that persons should seek, the actual selections of those values were subjective choices.

Rogers expressed supreme optimism in the ability of most individuals to make beneficial subjective choices by which to guide their own lives. Humans, he believed, were products of evolutionary development, and they therefore had an inbuilt ability to adjust to new circumstances and to meet new challenges. Therapists should regard "man as a process of becoming, as a process of achieving worth and dignity through the development of his potentialities." They should regard "the individual human being as a self-actualizing process, moving on to more challenging and enriching experiences."

Rogers's own views were remarkably adapted to the fast pace of mid-twentieth-century mainstream culture, where all traditions and dogmas were in question and the challenge was to adjust to the ever-accelerating rate of change. The American attitude, in the spirit of the postwar era, was very much that individuals, especially if aided by intelligence and technique, should be able to take control of their own destinies. Rogers's optimism resembled that of the great pragmatist and philosopher John Dewey when it came to his confidence in the ability of science to promote human advancement. Dewey, who also had a strongly religious background but had become secular, likewise preached a gospel of the human ability to use science to guide the evolutionary process so as to reach creativity and self-transcendence. "We find ourselves in fundamental agreement," wrote Rogers, "with John Dewey's statement: Science has made its way by releasing, not by suppressing, the elements of variation, of invention, and innovation, of novel creation in creatures."

Predictably, B. F. Skinner rejected Rogers's emphasis on creating autonomous, self-actualizing, free individuals. Internalized self-control was not the same as being free. "Even a pigeon can be taught some measure of self-control!" he said. Well-designed reinforcement techniques—like those used in effective parental training of children—did of course result in internalizing of controls. But the question for humans was, "Self-actualization—for what? Inner control is no more a goal than external." One had to determine the goals for which inner control would be used, and for that, science was needed. Ultimately, the goal had to be consistent with the evolutionary imperative of the "survival of mankind" or the "survival of my group." Not all the scientific facts were yet in for determining what were the best traits for that purpose, but as "transitional" values, said Skinner, he was "betting on the group [of investigators] whose practices make for healthy, happy, secure, productive and creative people." The important point for Skinner was that Rogers's focus on internal self-actualizing controls failed to take into account the external factors that might have created unhealthy goals for the individual. Suppose, for instance, "the client chooses the goal of becoming a more accomplished liar or murdering his boss." Either the factors that shaped the directions that self-actualization would take could be determined by an unregulated mix of traditions, practices,

myths, ideals, and interests, or they could be intelligently regulated by the best scientific thinking.[10]

As is often true of opponents in a given era, Skinner and
Rogers had more in common than they had differences.
Both saw humans and their cultures as rapidly evolving, and
both were interested in directing adjustments to that change.
Like those in the psychoanalytic tradition since Freud, neither
had any regard for traditional authority, but instead had concluded that natural science was the supreme external authority. Psychological theories and therapies existed mainly to help
people escape irrational controls from their past. Both Rogers
and Skinner had immense optimism regarding human nature
and in the malleability of human beings to be shaped or to
shape themselves for the better.

THE DEBATES OVER PSYCHOLOGICAL theory provide a
particularly sharp focus on the larger issues surrounding the
relationship between science and the individual that were
touching the lives of almost all Americans in very practical
ways. The twentieth century had become the age of the expert,
and that meant that people increasingly were looking to scientifically based knowledge for guidance on nearly every aspect
of their lives. Ever-improving technologies freed people from
lives of routine drudgery, but at the same time, those same
people were becoming increasingly dependent on experts, to tell
them not only how to use the technologies, but also how to
use their freedom. Life was guided not so much by traditional
moralities and mores but by learning how to cope with increasing numbers of choices among things to do, to enjoy, or

to avoid. Experts, in turn, were fortified with the latest scientific knowledge. Science and technical reasoning were supposed to enhance the freedom of individuals by allowing them to make their choices more intelligently.

The pervasiveness of new products, of new choices, and of expert advice on using them was multiplied by the commercial interests involved and the ever-present advertising. The classic case of how scientific authority might be mobilized to shape individual behavior was in cigarette advertising. In the early 1950s, the makers of Lucky Strike and Camel, two of the most popular brands, sent free samples to doctors and then vied with each other in their ads over which was preferred by the most physicians. So common were doctors in ads celebrating the health benefits of various brands that Old Gold, which tasted too strong to compete as healthful, countered with a long-standing ad: "If you want a Treat instead of a Treatment, smoke Old Gold." Chesterfield provided an archetypical combination of American reverence for both science and personal choice in its ads, depicting a scientist looking into a microscope while holding a cigarette in one hand: "SCIENCE discovered it. YOU can Prove it. No unpleasant after-taste." By the latter part of the 1950s, when health claims were being questioned, Viceroy, which touted a scientifically developed filter, also played the popular nonconformity card, saying, in its 1958 ad, "The Man who Thinks for Himself Knows . . . Only Viceroy has a thinking Man's Filter . . . a Smoking Man's Taste."

Experts were helping to change sexual mores as well. As had been true of most societies, in the United States of the 1950s there was a large gap between the professed public standards of morality and the actual behavior of ordinary people. Since at least the 1920s, one of the functions of the scientific expert had been to challenge restrictive conventional moralities. Freudianism, for instance, had been widely interpreted as an attack on sexual repression. Standard anthropological texts, such as Margaret Mead's *Coming of Age in Samoa* or Ruth Benedict's *Patterns of Culture*, helped relativize traditional Western assumptions about morality by showing that other societies thrived on very different views. In the postwar era, the most influential scientific studies reinforcing changing standards regarding sexuality were Alfred Kinsey's *Sexual Behavior in the Human Male*, published in 1948, and *Sexual Behavior in the Human Female*, published in 1953, together known as the Kinsey Reports. Both books, but especially the latter, because it discussed women, elicited a public outcry, a response that propelled the hefty volumes into becoming sensational best-sellers. The objections were not so much to the findings of the reports as to Kinsey's stance as the dispassionate scientific observer of the behavior of the human animal (he was a professor of zoology at Indiana University). What was entirely lacking in the reports, the critics pointed out, was any moral consideration. Rather, Kinsey documented that premarital and extramarital sex were not only commonplace, but might also be associated with health and happiness.[11]

The 1950s are sometimes thought of as being morally conservative—and in many ways they were, compared with what happened a generation later. But they can also be seen as a time of emerging permissiveness. World War II helped to loosen acceptable standards of behavior in all sorts of ways so that values were rapidly changing. The sexual revolution of the 1960s can be seen as an acceleration of trends that already were well under way. In 1953, Hugh Hefner launched *Playboy* magazine, propelled in its first issue by what became an iconic nude photograph of Marilyn Monroe. Some feared that publication of the photograph would ruin her movie career, but instead it helped to raise her to superstardom. Another sign of the times was that in 1956, Grace Metalious's first novel, *Peyton Place*, became a runaway best-seller, with more than 8 million copies in print by 1958. *Peyton Place*, like the Kinsey Reports, was not great literature, but it had a similar attraction in making public the kinds of sexual secrets, affairs, and premarital pregnancies that everyone knew about but was not supposed to talk about in small town America. By 1958, an American publisher dared to release Vladimir Nabokov's *Lolita*, the story of a middle-aged man's affair with a girl in her early teens. The novel, which was exceptional as literature, had been completed in 1953 but turned down by American publishers. It was published in France in 1956 but subsequently suppressed in both Great Britain and France. Yet it passed without censorship in the United States in 1958 and became yet another best-selling sensation. By the next year, a judge had allowed for the American publication of the original version of D. H. Lawrence's *Lady Chatterley's Lover*, a 1928 work that had long been banned as pornographic. American movies were still relatively tame, largely because of censorship that was especially responsive to Roman Catholic concerns, but by the end of the decade American public culture was on the verge of definitions of freedom that in a few years would include sexual freedom.[12]

Clearly, then, the experts did not create the revolution in mores. Rather, as was evident in the case of Kinsey, they simultaneously reflected the trends already in progress and provided them with scientifically based authority. Sexual mores were changing for many reasons, including increased social mobility, massive commercial interests that used sexual innuendo to sell products, and the simple propensities of human nature. Individual freedom was a long-standing ideal, and many people found it attractive to add sexual freedom to their list of natural rights. Nevertheless, scientific and social scientific studies were also providing sanctions for progressive views that said that individual self-determination was a preeminent value.

Arguably, the most influential expert in all of this was Dr. Benjamin Spock. His book *The Common Sense Book of Baby and Child Care*, first published in 1946, quickly became a best-seller, and eventually, "Dr. Spock," as the book was known, was seemingly the universal child-care book of the era. It was so widely recognized that it was used as the basis of a controversy between Lucy and Ricky on an *I Love Lucy* show. And like the other experts, he was providing scientific authority that both reflected and shaped America's increasingly individualistic mores.[13]

Dr. Spock was a particularly appealing scientifically based expert because he questioned the authority of experts. Child-rearing experts of the previous generation had promoted overly technical models for infant care, stressing the necessity of routine and discouraging old-fashioned instinctual practices, including breast-feeding. Dr. Spock's opening message,

"*Dr. Spock sure has your number!*"

Sydney Hoff, May 24, 1958, *The New Yorker*

by contrast, was quintessentially American and midcentury: "*Trust yourself.*" He assured new parents, in his preamble, "*You know more than you think you know.*" The experts may have calculated scientifically based routines for your child, but new parents should not be overwhelmed. They should trust their common sense. And the counterpart to trusting yourself was to trust your child. As if to counter any lingering Calvinism, Spock, a New Englander himself, assured readers, "Your baby is born to be a reasonable, friendly human being." That philosophy translated into advice to abandon the harsh methods of discipline that were often common in child rearing up to that time. Parents should not shame their children; spankings should be rare, at most; and far more could be accomplished by demonstrations of love than by punishment, which could create resentment and maladjustment. Dr. Spock's outlook included elements that combined B. F. Skinner and Carl Rogers. One should use positive reinforcement techniques, but also trust oneself and trust one's child.[14]

THESE TRENDS THAT WERE SO characteristic of the 1950s would have a lasting cultural impact. "Trust yourself" had been around at least since the days of Ralph Waldo Emerson, but at midcentury the advice came not just from exceptional individualists, but from almost everywhere, and with the authority of modern science. Social scientists of many stripes were proclaiming that conformity was the problem and nonconformity the solution, and so was almost everyone else, including contemporary artists, novelists, playwrights, poets, humanists, existentialists, and an assortment of pundits and clergy.

The meaning of life, everyone seemed to agree, could be found not by looking to tradition or to community, either past or present, but rather, by looking within. This midcentury consensus recommended that people free themselves, often with the authority of modern science, from traditionalist moralities and mythologies. Individual development, individuality, and self-fulfillment should be preeminent goals.

The resulting outlook has been nowhere better characterized than it was in the late 1970s by Christopher Lasch as "the culture of narcissism." Lasch, who came of age in the 1950s, grew up in a politically progressive family and spent his career critiquing the defects of the progressive liberal culture that had emerged since midcentury. Outlooks such as those of Carl Rogers were especially subject to his withering gaze.

"Economic man himself," he wrote, "has given way to the psychological man of our times—the final product of bourgeois individualism. The new narcissist is haunted not by guilt but by anxiety." By way of contrast, he said, nineteenth-century American individualism and the cult of success were not so much based on competition as on "an abstract ideal of discipline and self-denial." In the twentieth century, success became increasingly defined as victory over one's competitors, so that people "wish to be not so much esteemed as admired. They crave not fame but the glamour and excitement of celebrity." The new media greatly enhanced such attitudes. Advertising had created a culture in which people were more fascinated by images of things than they were by the things themselves.

Yet this new narcissistic culture, as Lasch described it, was not purely individualistic, because it also had to suit the needs of bureaucratic capitalism, which helped produce it. Bureaucratic culture (or that regulated in detail by administrators) came to favor the person who, much like David Riesman's "other-directed man" or William Whyte's "organization man," was skilled at manipulating personal relationships, but had no deep attachments. Society also developed what Lasch characterized as a "new paternalism"—directed by the expert, often supported by the government, and offering scientifically based advice on almost every conceivable dimension of human activity. B. F. Skinner might be seen as at least a minor prophet of that side of the culture. Almost every waking moment, in play as much as at work, in personal relationships, in home life, and in matters of health, was considered to be at its best when it was guided by the benevolent advice of the expert.[15]

As Lasch and others have observed, the two sides of the emerging culture, both narcissistic individualism and regulation by bureaucrats, are not as contradictory as they might seem, but can be complementary. When communities become almost entirely ad hoc—that is, they exist for particular limited purposes, whether for work, personal relationships, or recreation—the individual can reign supreme as at least in principle the designer of his or her own "lifestyle." Work may be governed by administrators and technical methodologies, but work also has the potential to provide one with the financial means and freedom to select one's own set of lifestyle activities. What frequently becomes problematic in this often attractive arrangement is the question of meaning. To what extent can meaning be found in the endless quest for competitive advancement, consumer goods, and entertainment? In a culture of self-fulfillment, what is actually fulfilling? As sociologist Robert Bellah and his coauthors wrote in their classic book *Habits of the Heart*, in describing the prevailing American culture as it had evolved by the 1980s, American culture revolved around two poles: the manager and the therapist. "The goal of living," observed Bellah, "is to achieve some combination of occupation and 'lifestyle' that is economically possible and psychically tolerable, that 'works.' The therapist, like the manager, takes the ends as they are given; the focus is on the effectiveness of the means." As Bellah put it, the "center is the autonomous individual, presumed able to choose the roles he will play and the commitments he will make, not on the basis of higher truths but according to the criterion of life-effectiveness as the individual judges it."[16]

At midcentury, two of the great ideals inherited from the enlightenment era—faith in scientific instrumental reason and faith in the individual—were among the most widely shared beliefs in the culture. In the upheavals of the late 1960s, many young people protested against the seeming contradictions of the two, as in countercultural outcries against the technocracy of capitalism and the military, against scientific planning and control, and against the myth of objectivity in Western linear thought—all in the name of individual freedom. But when after a few years members of the countercultural generation were settling down and getting jobs, they reentered a culture in which the two ideals, scientific instrumental reason and individualism, were both still alive and well. Rather than being shaped by a community or a tradition, people might choose their own lifestyle. In such a society, the two ideals could be complementary, at least practically speaking. In "the culture of narcissism," free individuals would be guided by the manager and the therapist.

FIVE

The Latter Days of the Protestant Establishment

AT THE SAME TIME THAT FAITH IN INDIVIDUAL AUTONOMY and the authority of science was standard fare in so much of midcentury American culture, the United States was experiencing one of the most widespread religious revivals in its history. Record numbers were attending religious services of almost every type and level, from those who went to tent revivalists for healing to prosperous old-line Protestants, from fans of Billy Graham to devotees of Reinhold Niebuhr, from hyper-biblicist sects to broad spiritualists, from the white and the black rural South to the urban ethnic neighborhoods of Roman Catholics or Jews, and including varieties of other Christian and non-Christian beliefs and practices. Millions read Rabbi Joshua Loth Liebman's 1946 number-one bestseller *Peace of Mind* and the Reverend Norman Vincent Peale's 1952 counterpart, *The Power of Positive Thinking*, both of which promised religiously based self-fulfillment. In 1952, a record 75 percent of Americans responding to pollsters said that religion was "very important" in their lives. And in 1957, more than four out of five affirmed that religion was not "old fashioned and out of date," but rather, "can answer today's problems." Between 1950 and 1960, church affiliation jumped an amazing 14 percent, going from 55 percent of the total population to 69 percent. By the end of the 1950s, attendance at religious services similarly reached an all-time peak.[1]

The intriguing question that emerges, then, is this: How did these two simultaneously huge cultural trends—the consensus outlooks celebrating both scientific authority and autonomy, and the religious revival—fit with each other? More broadly, how could a culture that was so modern, secular, and antitraditional in so many of its practices and ways of thinking be at the same time so religious? How did so much religion fit with the rest of the cultural mainstream? How such questions typically were addressed in the 1950s has important implications for the subsequent rise of the religious right by the late 1970s. They also lead into the culminating theme of this book: how best to accommodate a variety of religious viewpoints in pluralistic America.

THE STORY OF RELIGION in the 1950s has many dimensions, but at its center is the continuing heritage of cultural leadership of the mainline Protestant churches. These were the predominantly northern, white, Protestant denominations, such as Episcopal, Congregational (United Church of Christ), Presbyterian, American Baptist, United Methodist, Disciples of Christ, various sorts of Lutheran churches, and others, that were regarded as constituting an informal religious "establishment." That is, even though America had not had "established" state churches supported by taxes since its early days, Protestant Christianity still held a privileged place in the culture as the predominant religion. Mainline Protestant leaders were part of the liberal-moderate cultural mainstream, and their leading spokespersons were respected participants in the national conversation.

Protestantism had played a complementary role to more secular outlooks in public life throughout US history, and many Protestants were, of course, eager for this role to continue. It was a role that was embodied, for example, in the US Constitution. Written with remarkably little religious language for the time, the Constitution defined the federal government in a practically secular way. At the same time, the framers took care in the religion clauses of the First Amendment ("congress shall make no law respecting an establishment of religion, or prohibiting the free exercise thereof") to guarantee that religion might flourish in many supplemental capacities—even in tax-supported established churches in some New England states. Although the early republic was not a "Christian nation" in the sense that some conservative Christians today claim, neither was it wholly secular. Protestant Christianity retained many public privileges. Some of these were ceremonial and others were substantial. Education, which in Christendom had always had a conspicuous religious component, continued to include Protestant teachings. In the mid-nineteenth century, for instance, even state universities had required chapel attendance and were likely to have clergymen as presidents. Protestants could also form voting blocs large enough to shape religiously based legislation, as in Sabbath laws, or in promoting various social and moral reforms. The last great manifestation of that public influence was in the movement for prohibition of the sale of alcoholic beverages, culminating in the Eighteenth Amendment in 1919.

By the 1950s, although Protestants retained disproportional influence, the question loomed as to how such influence might continue. Prohibition itself had brought strong reactions against allowing one religious group to impose its restrictive teachings on everyone else. Moreover, as it was increasingly recognized that the nation included various religious, secular, and simply profane outlooks, the prospects for specific religious teachings to continue to play a role in shaping a public national consensus were looking increasingly problematic.

A PROMINENTLY PROPOSED SOLUTION to this problem was the one offered by Protestant "modernism." A modernist was one who saw God's work continuing to be revealed through the best developments of modern times. During the 1920s, American Protestantism became sharply divided between fundamentalists, who militantly insisted on holding onto strictly biblical teachings, and modernists, who believed that the best way to preserve Christianity was to allow it to grow with the best thought and moral ideals of the modern world.

The continuing influence of Protestant modernism in the 1950s might be illustrated by looking at various clergymen, theologians, and popular religious writers, but the best example is found in someone who was none of these, but far more influential: Henry Luce, head of the Time, Inc., publishing empire. The key to understanding Luce is that he was the child of Presbyterian missionaries, and he always remained a missionary to and for America. Born in China in 1898, he attended Yale in the World War I era. As a student he was active in Yale's famously evangelical Dwight Hall, where he sometimes preached. Although he remained religious after college, his views concerning the essence of Christianity had radically changed. In response to the challenges of modern science and modern thought, he abandoned more traditional forms of Christianity and emerged as a quintessential Protestant modernist. During the next decades, Luce continued to be an active lay Presbyterian, occasionally preaching to church and college groups. He used *Time* and *Life* to keep religion in the news, and he probably did as much as anyone in the era to sustain the idea that religion was still part of the American cultural mainstream. Although Luce's views were explicitly theistic, his application of them involved no consistent distinction between the church (and similar religious groups) and American society. America was, in effect, his church, and America's mission to the world was Henry Luce's Christian mission.[2]

In 1955, Luce's influential business magazine, *Fortune*, marked its twenty-fifth anniversary by publishing a series of articles by leaders in various fields speculating on what America would be like twenty-five years hence, in 1980. The projections concerning America's economic future were, as one might expect in 1955, exceedingly upbeat. Experts anticipated continuing economic growth that would lead to doubling in family incomes and a shortening of the workweek. As an aside, the most fascinating predictions concerned the

American energy situation in 1980. A number of the authors were confident about harnessing the atom for peaceful purposes. David Sarnoff, president of the Radio Corporation of America, wrote, for instance, "I do not hesitate to forecast that atomic batteries will be commonplace long before 1980," and that small atomic generators would be installed in homes. In another of the articles, John von Neumann of the Atomic Energy Commission went so far as to suggest that "a few decades hence energy may be free—just like unmetered air."[3]

Luce himself contributed the culminating article, which was on religion. Luce reflected on how religious and material progress might continue to go hand in hand. He recognized that the nation in 1955 was in some ways undergoing a cultural crisis that conceivably could have demoralizing consequences. "Science," he wrote, "discloses no 'meaning' or 'purpose.'" Moreover, "our artists and our novelists have disintegrated the human personality into the miserable shreds of degradation." Americans overwhelmingly continued to have an immense regard for "human dignity" and still believed that life had purpose. Yet a haunting question remained: "Is our talk a last collective shout in a cosmic graveyard?" he asked. "Twenty-five years from now, will men believe still that there is in life a 'dignity' infinitely precious—that liberty wagered against death will win and is forever worth winning?" Luce believed that the strength of America was that most of her citizens still accepted the Christian idea that life's purpose was God-given. "Our acceptance of the Christian answer," he conceded, "is apt to be careless, shallow and ignorant, both in theory and in practice; but it is the one we are used to; it is the one which, despite our quarrels and uproars, has given to American life and politics a remarkable *consensus*." He also believed that the consensus was based on a widely shared sense of divinely instituted principles. At almost the same time as he penned his *Fortune* article, he used a university address to respond to Walter Lippmann's call for a basis for a public philosophy. "Mr. Lippmann," said Luce, "writes as a pessimist, I speak as an optimist." His answer to the dour Lippmann was simply that America already had a public philosophy, one that only recently had been reiterated by President Eisenhower himself, who had proclaimed that the nation's laws were "rooted in moral law, respecting a religious faith that man is created in the image of God."[4]

The central question facing Americans, Luce emphasized in his *Fortune* speculations, was whether they would preserve their publicly shared faith in the face of the intellectual and social challenges of the coming era. Continuing growth and change in response to new challenges was the essence of the Protestant modernist agenda. Christianity, Luce assured his readers, would endure to the end of time, yet it would have to adjust to changing civilization in order to do so. Luce cited the missionary slogan that "the gospel must be preached in every tongue," but interpreted it to mean that "*it must be preached in the different language of every different age.*" The great intellectual challenge to the faith in the early twentieth century had been modern science. But America, Luce assured, had moved beyond the Scopes trial and its false choice of science *or* religion. The consensus now, he believed, was that science and religion were not in conflict but simply "two distinct worlds" with correspondingly distinct standards. That recognition had brought peace between science and religion. The next step was to bring cooperation. That was what Luce foresaw, or at least that is what he hoped for: that by 1980, there would be a new view of man in "collaboration with God in the whole of evolution."[5]

Henry Luce's hopes that by 1980 most Americans would share a common faith proved almost as far off the mark as the *Fabulous Future* predictions that energy would become virtually free. In Luce's case, he was projecting the theological modernist hope into the future. That hope was that the essence of true theism, derived largely but not exclusively from the Christian heritage, would serve as a higher point of reference in guiding the United States as the country led Western civilization and the world in "the American century." That shared faith would be pluralistic in the sense characteristic of the 1950s, in that it would be inclusive of peoples of many subfaiths. For Luce and for many of his generation, such a growing inclusive pluralism fit their experience. Religion had not declined, as many during the cultural crisis of the 1920s had predicted it would. Public expressions of a common faith were growing. Yet the sort of shared, generically Christian/American religion that Luce was projecting into the future was already too problematic to long endure as a substantial part of American public life.

THE FACT WAS THAT despite the religious revival taking place at almost every level, American culture of the 1950s was simultaneously strikingly secular. "Secular" here means only that most activities were conducted without direct religious reference, not that they were necessarily antireligious. For instance, religious faith had only tangential influences throughout the economic system or in typical workplaces, huge areas of the culture. Furthermore, growing dependence on technology created other vast areas of technical activity that by their nature had little to do with faith. As the French sociologist-philosopher Jacques Ellul would soon be pointing out, "technique" had to do not only with literal technology but also with the technological principle that determined so much of modern activity in culture, business, and even sports. That driving principle was the search for the most rational and efficient means of getting a job done. So a modern corporation, for instance, might as a matter of course uproot "personnel," with no regard for family, religious, or community considerations, and move them to a distant city, because that was the most efficient way to maximize profits. Moreover, if what is considered important to pass on to the next generation is an index of the priorities of a civilization, it is revealing that religious considerations had almost nothing to do with the subject matter taught in public schools. Even most religious people were content to supplement secular public-school teachings merely with a twenty-minute Sunday-school lesson. In higher education, religion could be studied as an area of special interest, but it was rarely considered as a possible norm or even as a point of reference regarding the vast majority of what was taught. Indeed, the dominant public discourse of the era that we have been considering was conducted mostly without religious reference. Faith was sometimes a matter of controversy that entered into politics and the news, but most often it was treated as a special interest, so that even in Henry Luce's *Time*, where it sometimes rated a cover story, it was otherwise confined to its own section, beside leisure, sports, and the arts.[6]

The paradox of having so many religious people participating in a culture so detached from religious concerns is best described in terms of the "privatization" of religion. In diverse modern societies, privatization is the most common way of dealing with traditional religious faiths. In the religiously diverse United States, it has typically been considered fine to practice a specific religious faith as a private option, but one's faith is not supposed to intrude in any substantive way into the spheres of one's public activities. Some degree of privatization seems almost necessary in a highly diverse society in which many activities are technologically defined. Privatization helps people to cooperate in public activities. Since the late twentieth century, privatization has been conspicuously the dominant (though far from unchallenged) way of dealing with religious diversity. What is less recognized, at least in popular perceptions, is the degree to which privatization was already far advanced in the very religious 1950s.

The extent of privatization during that decade was obscured by its incompleteness. There was still enough regard for religious expression in public for it to seem as if faith were integral to national life. World War II, the Cold War, and the religious revival had temporarily slowed the longer-term trends toward privatization. Even some very traditional religious viewpoints were getting good press in a way they had not in the 1920s or 1930s. Billy Graham is the outstanding instance. He had the ear of presidents and, despite his essentially fundamentalist gospel, had made his peace with the mainline Protestant establishment. He was a major voice to be heard on public issues. That popularity overshadowed the fact that most of the preachers who proclaimed such a born-again message—even some with very large followings, such as Pentecostal Oral Roberts—were clearly cultural outsiders with no such voice. Catholics had also gained in mainstream recognition and respectability since World War II. Despite some renewal of anti-Catholicism marked by Paul Blanshard's 1949 best-seller, *American Freedom and Catholic Power*, by the end of the 1950s relations between mainline Protestants and Catholics had thawed. At the popular level, Bishop Fulton Sheen's TV show, *Life Is Worth Living*, in which he explained Catholic doctrine with a dramatic flair, became one of the most popular shows of the era. And the progressive Catholic priest Father John Courtney Murray received much favorable attention for his essays in *We Hold These Truths: Catholic Reflections on the American Proposition*, published in 1960 when Senator John F. Kennedy, a Catholic, was running for president. In addition, major mainline Protestant theologians, of whom Reinhold Niebuhr and Paul Tillich were the best known, consistently commanded significant attention in the national conversation. All of these made the cover of *Time* magazine.[7]

These conspicuous public expressions could make it seem that some sort of shared religious faith was alive and well and might have a bright future even as it became more inclusive. The mainline Protestant establishment seemed in many ways to be thriving. All the biggest and oldest denominations were growing. The National Council of Churches provided a prominent public voice for mainline Protestants. Nonetheless, that degree of cooperation also obscured the extent to which American Protestantism was in fact deeply and often sharply divided between North and South, white and black, Anglo old-stock versus newer ethnic, and inclusive mainline versus exclusive and often separatist fundamentalist, conservative evangelicals and Pentecostals. Many of these had no public voice, except perhaps locally.

Such divisions, and the degree of privatization they fostered, were also obscured by a compensating increase in generalized public religious affirmations, especially of an undefined common theism. The Cold War was widely perceived as a battle against "godless communism." For many Americans, including American leaders, that was not simply a rhetorical issue. President Harry S. Truman and President Dwight D. Eisenhower, as well as many leading diplomats, regarded the conflict with the atheistic Soviet Union as involving a spiritual conflict.[8] President Eisenhower, moreover, was especially effective in promoting what later became known as American "civil religion" as a way of strengthening a consensus of domestic resolve in the struggle against communism. Civil religion is a popular piety that treats the nation itself as an object of worship. It involves engaging in symbolic rituals, such as honoring the flag and observing national holidays, as well as hallowing the memories of great leaders. In the 1950s, such shared national piety played a significant role in building a sense of consensus. In 1954, Congress reinforced the popularity of such trends by adding "under God" to the Pledge of Allegiance, and two years later it adopted "In God we trust" as the national motto.

Such acts of national piety strengthened a sense that the nation's religious heritage was doing just fine, despite a lot of evidence that could have been interpreted to the contrary. American disestablishment of religion had allowed room for formal religious expression even within the government and public schools. The US Congress as well as state legislatures and many public events were opened with predominantly Protestant invocations. In public schools, Bible reading and Christian prayers were common. Public school Christmas programs were likely to be largely Christian, and schools sponsored Christian baccalaureate services for graduating seniors. Many localities maintained Sunday "blue laws," such as prohibiting the sale of alcohol on that day, as a continuing expression of Protestant privilege. Most of these religious expressions were leftovers of the era of Christendom, but the fact that they were still in place signaled a formal respect for that heritage.

In popular culture, even though entertainment was overwhelmingly secular, there was enough public celebration of religion and room for religious options to make it seem at least religion-friendly. Celebrities spoke sentimentally of "the man upstairs." Film star and sex symbol Jane Russell famously characterized God as a "livin' doll." Movies typically cast Catholic priests as manly and caring.[9] Religion also sold well, so film spectacles, such as *Ben Hur*, *The Ten Commandments*, and *The Robe*, became blockbuster hits. "He's Got the Whole World in His Hands," performed by the English singer Laurie London, reached number one on the hits charts in 1958. Elvis Presley's Christmas album, which included one side of religious numbers, became an all-time best-seller. The combination of widespread religious practice and public religious expression created a sense that religion was fundamental to American life, or at least should be.

The superficialities of much of this common public faith did not go unnoticed at the time, especially by those who held out for the more specific faith of a particular religion. The most influential work calling attention to the tensions between these two kinds of faith was Will Herberg's sociologically based study *Protestant-Catholic-Jew*, published in 1955. Herberg had gone through the requisite radical phase of intellectuals of his generation, but had been influenced by Reinhold Niebuhr and had become conservative regarding both religion and culture. Being Jewish himself, he celebrated that Catholics and Jews were becoming part of the American mainstream, but he believed it was at the price of effectively subordinating their traditional religious beliefs and practices to the *operative* religion of most Americans, "the American Way of Life." That operative shared religion included faith in the dignity of the individual, the superiority of American democracy, and the pragmatic doctrine of "deeds not creeds." It thus turned religion from being the highest value into an instrument for promoting other values that in practice proved to be a person's higher concerns. Many Americans who professed faith neither knew nor cared much about the particulars of their religious tradition.[10]

Martin Marty, a young Lutheran scholar, offered further insights into the situation in *The New Shape of American Religion*, which appeared in 1959. The so-called revival of religion, Marty explained, was largely a revival of "interest in religion."

Unlike earlier American awakenings, this one was not primarily a renewal of Protestantism but "*a maturing national religion.*" And this national religion, which was shared even by many of the unchurched, was strikingly vague. Most Americans seemed to be in favor of a God of "religion-in-general." Marty quoted Eugene Carson Blake, president of the National Council of Churches, who had characterized this religion as "America's humanistic nationalism." "This ideology is what an American is if nobody tampers with his attitudes," said Blake. "His articles of faith are science (in its engineering applications), common sense (his own ideas), the Golden Rule (in its negative form), sportsmanship, and individual independence." Blake called this faith "humanism" not because such Americans did not believe in God, but because God for them served as a sort of useful ally in support of these beliefs.[11]

The problem, as Marty himself framed it, was a variation on the theme of the decade: conformity. Even Americans who were active in churches, said Marty, were likely to subordinate their professed traditional theological beliefs to the pervasive national creed. Americans had built a consensus around a "religion of democracy." They often blended their traditional religious beliefs with faith in America. President Eisenhower's typical utterances, such as "A democracy cannot exist without a religious base," reinforced this blending. The underlying beliefs of most Americans, even though they might be expressed in Christian terms, were essentially "secular and humanistic." Their humanism could be found not only in their faith in democratic government, but also in the self-help faith of a Norman Vincent Peale and in general affirmations that religious faith was a step toward wholeness and self-fulfillment. Belief in nonconformity had become the new conformity. So church people, ironically, often conformed to the prevailing secular American ideals of autonomy and individuality. These ubiquitous ideals of an "independent, individualistic or autonomous man" were essentially secular, as they owed more to America's enlightenment heritage than they did to its Christian background. "'Enlightenment' man," declared Marty, was "behind much of the Protestant compulsion to create a new individualism."[12]

IF, AS HERBERG, MARTY, and many others were pointing out, characteristic American religious belief often intersected with the mainstream culture in ways that only reinforced essentially secular trends, what was the alternative? In answering that question, no one was more often cited as a prophetic counterexample than Reinhold Niebuhr. Will Herberg and Martin Marty were both admirers of Niebuhr. Martin Luther King Jr. was also significantly shaped by Niebuhr, and in turn helped to show how African American Christianity could be the most conspicuous exception to any claims of insubstantial religious influence in public life. So wide was Niebuhr's influence, not only in mainline Protestant churches but even among liberal intellectuals, that Harvard philosopher Morton White tagged a significant contingent of his followers as "atheists for Niebuhr."[13]

Niebuhr's reputation was well deserved. He was one of the most important thinkers of the twentieth century, and he is well worth studying today. He taught at Union Theological

Seminary in New York, just across the street from Columbia University, and thus was near the epicenter of American cultural life. As a prophetic voice he was most effective in challenging the assumptions underlying both of the great ideals of the day, faith in science and faith in self-determination. The underlying assumption in both cases was optimism about the ability of humans to control their own destinies. Niebuhr countered that optimism by rehabilitating the Christian doctrine of "original sin." At the core of the human condition was an egotism marked by a tendency to think too highly of oneself. Freedom, or the ability to transcend the determination of mere natural forces, was what distinguished humans from the beasts. But humans also had an inbuilt tendency to mistake that transcendence for an autonomy in which they viewed themselves as captains of their own destinies. Especially striking in Niebuhr's analysis of original sin was the idea that humans were corrupted not only by their open vices, but just as much by their virtues and accomplishments, which became sources of their pride. Niebuhr was a master of the telling paradox. "A too confident sense of justice," he characteristically observed, "always leads to injustice." Everyone, individuals as well as nations, needed to be humbled, and to be humbled they had to see themselves from a larger perspective, ultimately from the divine perspective.[14]

One implication of the doctrine of original sin, or of ineradicable human egotism, was Niebuhr's "realism" in human affairs, which included his insistence that force might be necessary to counter evil. The twentieth century had proven that political problems could not be solved simply by goodwill and scientifically based social engineering. So for many, Niebuhr's realism was a welcome antidote to the superficial optimism of utopian, romantic, and scientifically based promises to move the race toward perfection.

Niebuhr's popularity among so many thoughtful observers reveals a side of the 1950s that is sometimes overlooked. Despite the upbeat character of much of the culture of postwar America, despite the popularity of Norman Vincent Peale and "trust yourself" psychology, despite all the recommendations for autonomy, there was another strong undertow pulling in the opposite direction, suggesting there might be a fundamental flaw in the human condition. The twentieth century illustrated unprecedented dimensions of human brutality and "inhumanity" and great propensities toward self-deception in turning ideologies into blinding absolutes. The prevailing American optimism and self-confidence were undercut by uncertainties and anxieties born of historical realities as well as by the ever-present possibility of atomic holocaust. Niebuhr's works resonated with many literary works, too, such as those of William Faulkner, Tennessee Williams, and Flannery O'Connor, who depicted deep-seated and seemingly irremediable human failings. Niebuhr often invoked the Jewish and Christian heritage of recognizing that humans were inherently sinful and therefore needed to depend on God. Nonetheless, as Morton White observed, many of his readers could accept his insights on the paradoxes of human nature while ignoring the theological ground of his arguments.[15]

Niebuhr's popularity in the liberal-moderate mainstream of the 1950s was heightened by his insightful book *The Irony of*

American History. Appearing in 1952 when McCarthyism was at its height, when the United States was still fighting in Korea, and when the conflict with communism and the Soviets was being described in simple black-and-white terms, Niebuhr's analysis seemed like a breath of fresh air. He could speak with a degree of moderation because he was already established as firmly anti-Communist and known for his "realism" in foreign policy, especially his argument that force must be met with force.

Yet even though Niebuhr deplored Soviet totalitarianism, he also pointed out what to many readers was an illuminating insight: that the United States had more in common with the Soviet Union than either would be willing to admit. Each affirmed the goal that humans should be masters of their own destinies. Each believed that the prescription for reaching that goal involved following the dictates of an economic system. Each had a myth of its own innocence and of the corruption of its opponents. It was particularly ironic that while Americans saw their prosperity as evidence of God's favor and hence of their own virtue, their enemies saw Americans' riches as evidence of their vice. Americans were fond of condemning the Soviet Union's "materialism," Niebuhr observed, "but we are rather more successful practitioners of materialism as a working creed than the communists, who have failed so dismally in raising the general standards of well-being." Each nation saw itself in the forefront of modern progress based on the highest intellectual authority: the scientific analysis of social conditions. Each was a latter-day manifestation of the enlightenment faith in the ability of science and rationality to solve human problems. Each nation continued to have an almost unreserved regard for the scientific model as the key to controlling and improving the human condition.[16]

In detailing the American version of naïve faith in the natural scientific method for engineering social progress, one of Niebuhr's favorite targets was John Dewey. According to Niebuhr, Dewey was just the most prominent priest in a widespread cult of faith in human intelligence. In *The Irony of American History*, Niebuhr quoted a letter to the journal *Science* in which an unnamed writer deployed a common argument of the day, that "if men can come to understand and control the atom, there is reasonable likelihood that they can in the same way learn and control human group behavior." Niebuhr saw such assumptions as pervading the social sciences, and he had long regarded Dewey as one of the most influential purveyors of the false hope that the scientific method that worked so well for understanding nature was therefore the best guide for human behavior.[17]

Niebuhr's critique of faith in the ability of human intelligence to control history was based on an essential distinction, or dualism, in his thought between the realm of nature and the realm of history. Nature was the realm of necessity and was therefore susceptible to scientific investigation and control. But history was the realm of freedom as well as natural causes. Even at the level of natural causation much of human behavior was insusceptible to prediction and control, because causal chains were operating simultaneously at so many levels: "geologic, geographic, climatic, psychological, social, and personal." In addition, and more importantly, "human agents intervene unpredictably in the course of events," and even when they were just trying to observe events, they remained as interested actors. Human self-interested perversity could also subvert the best-laid prescriptions. One only had to witness the Soviet Union to find the outstanding examples of this human inability to manage history according to a scientific scheme. Pragmatic American social scientists were preferable in that they rejected global ideologies, and their methods yielded some real benefits. Yet, as humans characteristically did, they overestimated the relatively good. Hence, their belief that the scientific method was the key to resolving human social and political problems was ultimately naïve.[18]

The intensity of Niebuhr's disagreement with Dewey and pragmatic social scientists is best understood as, in a sense, a family quarrel. Niebuhr, too, was an avowed pragmatist. He had been deeply influenced by William James, and he broadly followed James's method of preserving a realm of freedom above the determinism of mere nature. In typical pragmatist fashion, Niebuhr held that "things and events are in a vast web of relationships and are known through their relations." Trying to understand reality in all its relationships helped him guard against ethics that absolutized the relative. Niebuhr was instead characteristically occupied with discovering the relatively best solutions that lay between extremes. Like James, but unlike Dewey, Niebuhr believed that the meaningful relationships in reality included religious experiences and categories that went beyond nature alone. These theistic perspectives were essential to determining one's ideals and also to appreciating one's limitations in meeting those ideals. Unlike James,

Niebuhr drew on explicitly Christian theological categories that emphasized human finitude, sinfulness, and dependence, and so he was critical of James's optimism. Furthermore, and very much like Dewey, Niebuhr went beyond James's individualism and applied the pragmatic method to the project of establishing an American social ethic. Yet he had a sharp falling out with strictly secular pragmatists who followed Dewey in believing that modern science could provide the highest authority for constructing such a social ethic.[19]

Niebuhr made sure to emphasize that he did not reject natural science or the natural scientific method as such. Like many mainline Protestants of the generation that had witnessed the Scopes trial of 1925, he was at pains to assure his readers that, whatever his critiques of naïve liberalism, he was not anything like a fundamentalist. "If we take the disciplines of the various sciences seriously, as we do," he affirmed, "we must depart at one important point from the biblical picture of life and history." In positing a dualism between nature and freedom, Niebuhr was conceding that the realm of nature was determined, and hence that the dictates of natural science indeed reigned supreme there. "The accumulated evidence of the natural sciences convinces us that the realm of natural causation is more closed, and less subject to divine intervention, than the biblical world view assumes." Accordingly, "we" [meaning sophisticated moderns] "do not believe in the virgin birth, and we have difficulty with the physical resurrection of Christ. We do not believe, in other words, that revelatory events validate themselves by a divine break-through in the natural order." Contrary to those who took the Bible literally,

Niebuhr argued that the truths of revelation were better understood simply as essential verities, rather than on the basis of historical facts validated by miracles. The truth of the revelation of the fall of humanity, for instance, was too profound to be dependent on belief in literal events in the Garden of Eden. The same would apply to other biblical doctrines. They had some relation to history in that they fit human experience, but they were not dependent on biblical claims of literal divine interventions in the course of nature.[20]

Niebuhr thus was careful to grant scientific outlooks sovereignty in their own territories, even as he resisted imperialistic efforts to reduce human experience to naturalistic terms. Such scientific imperialism failed to take account of the realm of freedom in human history, the realm in which genuine encounters with God were possible. Niebuhr had thus reserved a place in modern culture for what he regarded as the essence of Christian faith, a place that would be safe from the onslaughts of scientific naturalism. Within that sanctuary, one could benefit from scientific findings and use reason as well as the history of human religious experience as a guide for identifying the best of shared human insights into the divine. Yet how one interpreted or chose among those insights also depended to a degree on subjective human experience.

The grand irony of that strategy was that, while Niebuhr himself used it effectively as a way to preserve a public role for the Christian heritage, its subjective qualities made the faith wholly optional and dispensable. As atheists for Niebuhr evidenced, one could simply bypass the theology and adopt the profound insights into human limitations that Niebuhr offered.[21] Niebuhr was remarkable in that he was a Protestant theologian who could speak to a wide swath of American liberal culture. Yet he was also speaking at the end of the Protestant era, and for all his brilliance was like a candle that burns brightest just before it goes out.

ALTHOUGH NIEBUHR'S INSIGHTS had significant impact on cultural leaders here and there, his sort of theology could not even begin to deflect one of the most conspicuous forces of his era, a force that he himself identified—modern culture's growing secularity. In 1957, for the one hundredth anniversary issue of *Atlantic Monthly*, he described those forces with characteristic perceptiveness in an essay on "Pious and Secular America." The United States, he observed, was "at once the most religious and the most secular of Western nations." His question was, "How shall we explain this paradox?"

In answering this question, Niebuhr distinguished two very different sorts of forces shaping America's burgeoning modern secularity. One kind of secularity was "a theoretical secularism which dismisses ultimate questions about the meaning of existence, partly because it believes that science has answered these questions and party because it regards the questions as unanswerable or uninteresting." The other secularizing force was "a practical secularism, which expresses itself in the pursuit of the immediate goals of life," and which America's detractors characterized as "materialism." That second kind of secularity arose from "our passion for technical efficiency," a passion that, when combined with abundant natural resources, provided America with a cornucopia. Although American piety

"Miss Lewis, Quick! Get me Dial-A-Prayer!"

Perry Barlow, March 5, 1960, *The New Yorker*

had always had some impact on American political culture, it had had almost no impact on its economic culture, where the demands of efficient technique overwhelmed all else.

Niebuhr thought both kinds of secularity could be compatible with religion retaining a real place in American life. Ever since the American Revolution, the secular heirs of the enlightenment and the religious heirs of frontier revivalism had been able to agree on many shared ideals, even if most of these involved a shared naïveté and optimism regarding human abilities. And in the contemporary world crisis, it was not hard to see the limits of "the enlightened mind," and the fact "that great technical power cannot solve these ultimate problems of human existence." Hence, Americans were finding that "the frame of meaning, established by the traditionally historic religions, has become much more relevant to the modern man than seemed possible a century ago." Underneath all the prosperity and expressions of confidence was an emptiness. "Our gadget-filled paradise suspended in a hell of international insecurity," he proclaimed in a particularly arresting phrase, "certainly does not offer us even the happiness of which the former century dreamed." Niebuhr believed that most of the revived religion of the day did not adequately face this reality, but he also thought there was still hope that a gospel that was more realistic about human limitations might prevail. So, he continued: "Only when we realize these disappointed hopes can we have a truly religious culture. It will probably disappoint the traditionally pious as much as the present paradise disappoints the children of the Enlightenment."

What is striking in this essay is the disparity between the profundity of the diagnosis and the superficiality of the prescription. In part that may be attributed to the popular nature of the article, but it also is revealing of the problem of a lack of a source of authority to which to appeal beyond the weight of Niebuhr's own insights into selected biblical themes. So he concluded his account of how America might find a "truly religious culture" with an appeal only to a "piety [that] will have recaptured some of the characteristic accents of the historic religions." But this recapturing, he made clear, would also alter those religions. Tellingly, he spoke of them in the past tense. "The great historic religions, in short," he declared in his culminating sentence, "were rooted in the experience of the ages so that they could not be deluded by the illusions of a technical age." Niebuhr was pointing to some sort of higher synthesis of the greatest principles from higher religious heritages as the last best hope for an improved American faith. He was not as optimistic as Henry Luce, but he, too, was proposing a modernized theism, even if a chastening theism. No more than Luce did he offer any suggestion as to how such a higher theology might even begin to gain currency sufficient to counter the secularizing trends that he had identified with such insight.[22]

What neither Luce nor Niebuhr could see was how near they were to the end of an era. The United States had been shaped by an alliance between enlightenment rationality and Protestant religion. Since the days of the early republic, there had always been room for an informal religious establishment to play an occasionally significant supplemental role, even as most of the business, politics, learning, literature, and arts of the nation were conducted on essentially secular grounds. That arrangement still seemed to be flourishing throughout the 1950s, especially in the midst of such widespread religious resurgence. Yet, two decades later, after the cultural upheaval of the late 1960s, the idea of a mainline Protestant establishment was hardly more than a memory.

Although Niebuhr, in contrast to Luce, cautioned against thinking of America as a "Christian" nation or as a nation especially chosen by God, he did insist that the Judeo-Christian heritage provided uniquely valuable resources for shaping public policy. His chastening theology thus provided a way for sophisticated Protestants to carry on the project of Christianizing the social order, even while acknowledging their own limits. So they still took for granted that essentially Protestant principles should play a special role in shaping the nation as a whole.[23]

Part of the problem in sustaining such an outlook would be the prevailing midcentury conception of pluralism as meaning primarily inclusive pluralism. Most mainline Protestant spokespersons shared this consensus-oriented ideal with their more secular counterparts. To be fully pluralistic meant to be not too dogmatic, to be open to learning from a variety of viewpoints, and to be looking for ideals that had proved themselves empirically in the crucible of the modern era and could be widely shared. Even though traditional Christian doctrines might guide the way, religious truth, like other truth, was developing and progressive. That meant that if Christianity was to retain a substantial public influence, Christians would have to deemphasize divisive dogmas and emphasize the essential truths and moral teachings that were compatible with progressive scientific thinking and acceptable in a pluralistic setting. Yet, that strategy left unanswered the question of why enlightened progressive Christianity should be privileged over any other teachings, whether secular or religious.

When that inequity was pointed out, often stridently, in the attacks of the 1960s on the White Anglo-Saxon Protestant (WASP) establishment, mainline Protestants were, to their credit, often among the first to recognize the point. Yet their retreat, sometimes in the name of celebrations of "the secular," did not leave in its wake any new sensibility that pluralism might involve encouraging a variety of religiously informed voices in public life. Rather, the new diversity was dedicated to ensuring that various groups defined in essentially secular terms—such as race, ethnicity, gender, or sexual preference—were equally represented in the public domain. Diverse religious voices were to be tolerated, but they were regarded as private options, not as significant points of view that ought to contribute to the public domain.

So as the public role of mainline Protestantism was rapidly diminishing, the mainstream culture had no provision for encouraging a wider variety of religiously informed views in its place. Ever since the American Revolution, mainline Protestantism had maintained whatever sacred canopy there was that hung over the nation to provide religious legitimacy for public mores.[24] Often that canopy had been torn and tattered and provided only superficial coverage. Yet it had great symbolic significance. So, even as that old sacred canopy was being hauled down during the retreat of mainline Protestantism in the 1960s and 1970s, others rushed in, attempting to raise another in its place.

The effort by the religious right to create, in effect, a new informal Christian establishment, based on a "Christian consensus," is the subject of the next chapter. The resulting "culture wars" made it especially difficult to dispassionately address the question of religious pluralism in public life—which is the subject of the reflections in the conclusion.

SIX

Sequel: Consensus Becomes a Fighting Word

BY THE EARLY 1960S, THE ERA OF THE WHITE MALE Protestant and secular cultural leadership was in its last days. Midcentury hopes for a moderate-liberal cultural consensus were about to be blown away by the cultural upheavals and fragmentation of the later 1960s. The civil rights movement, and its aftermath of frustrations, opened the door to new forms of interest politics and to conflicting demands regarding diversity and inclusivism. No longer could it be taken for granted that white males would hold a near monopoly on cultural leadership. The American enlightenment ideal of a consensus based on rationally derived, shared humanistic principles congenial to a broadly theistic Protestant heritage was falling apart. The Vietnam War disrupted Cold War harmony regarding patriotism. The counterculture took to the streets with calls for nonconformity and for rejection of the depersonalizing effects of mass culture, thereby bringing down the monopoly on cultural authority of the generation's elders, who a decade earlier had been politely urging those same themes.

One of the most intriguing and momentous manifestations of the cultural fragmentation that followed the consensus era was the rise of the religious right in the late 1970s and its continuance ever since as a major player in the politics of the culture wars. That development is particularly striking because, during the 1950s, Christian fundamentalists themselves, along with other revivalist or conservative evangelical Protestants, typically prided themselves on their lack of political involvement. Most revivalist and conservative evangelical Protestants were simply Bible-believing Christians who emphasized being "born again"; the "fundamentalists" could be defined as those who were more militant—even, at times, "ultramilitant"—in fighting perceived doctrinal and moral evils.[1] In reaction to the "social gospel" of more liberal Protestants earlier in the century, revivalist conservatives often emphasized that the only concerns of the church and the evangelists should be to preach a gospel of salvation. They might promise, as Billy Graham did, social and political benefits for a nation of converted people, but they also held that direct involvement of churches in politics would be a distraction from their primary evangelistic task. Not everyone in the very diverse revivalist movement consistently followed such standards; even Graham himself did not observe them strictly. Revivalist Protestants were agreed in their anticommunism, and they often made comments on specific political issues, as individuals, in publications, or through organizations such as the National Association of Evangelicals. Sometimes they mobilized at the local level—for example, over what was being taught in the public schools. Wealthy evangelical businessmen helped to finance conservative political causes and urged their fellow believers to do the same. So it is easy enough to find anticipations of later political involvement. Nonetheless, at midcentury most revivalist Protestants were ardent premillennialists who held that the world was getting worse and that the only true hope for rescue from pervasive evil was the imminent personal return of Jesus Christ to set up his millennial kingdom on earth for a literal 1,000 years. Political programs, they often said, were like rearranging the deck chairs on the *Titanic*. Accordingly, they were probably less concerned with practical politics than most other Americans were. Nor were they unified in most of their political views or in their party allegiances. The well-worn critique that liberal Protestants made of revivalist evangelicals was that their gospel was too privatized and otherworldly.

Reflections on the cultural crisis of the 1950s shed light on the dynamics of the remarkable transformation of revivalist Protestantism from a mostly apolitical phenomenon into a formidable political force. Of course, many elements were involved in shaping the religious right, and the movement already has been viewed from many helpful angles.[2] Nevertheless, viewing the dramatic politicization of the fundamentalist-evangelical heritage through the lens of the preceding "consensus" era can provide some fresh perspectives on today's most persistent cultural divisions.

HISTORICAL CHANGE IS, of course, driven by a host of factors, some of which are beyond anyone's control. So understanding the shared beliefs of cultural leaders in the 1950s provides only one angle among many for assessing the reasons for change. That angle does tell us, for example, some important things about the ideological resources a mainstream culture may have for responding to new challenges and for shaping culture-forming institutions such as education, the media, and government. In these cases, we find that mostly secular moderate-liberal cultural leaders had little to offer beyond piecemeal solutions to the cultural challenges that they identified, and even less to offer to counter the unanticipated challenges of fragmentation that would begin to emerge in the next decade.

It is not hard to see why the center could not hold. Even in its heyday in the 1950s, centrist liberalism had been largely dependent on pragmatism, broadly speaking. Indeed, one of the claims of the day was that the culture had reached the historical stage that Daniel Bell had tagged "the end of ideology"—and this was seen as a sign of American progress. Pragmatism itself was a sort of ideology, or broad set of beliefs, but the point was that its flexible approaches to social issues were superior to rigid ideological approaches. That basic point seemed to be confirmed by the collapse of world communism later in the century. But the problem with pragmatism is that, although it can work admirably when it can draw on shared moral capital, it does not provide much basis for establishing first principles or deciding among contending moral claims. That failing became evident by the late 1960s, when numerous competing and often strident interest groups each presented the first principles of their respective causes as self-evident. The pragmatist has little basis for adjudicating among such claims when they conflict. Furthermore, in a consumer economy where the popular media constantly promote a culture of free choice and self-indulgence as the essence of the good life, the pragmatist has difficulty finding a widely compelling moral basis for alternatives.

These problems of moderate-liberal pragmatism were already discernible in the 1950s. Walter Lippmann, for instance, pointed them out when he called for a return to some sort of natural law as the basis for a public philosophy. His establishment critics responded by pointing out that such a return was impractical because there was no way to determine whose first principles should count as laws. In the setting of the 1950s, shoring up the foundations of public policy did not seem to them an urgent matter, because the public culture already enjoyed a remarkable de facto sense of unity. That sense of unity had been generated by World War II patriotism, Cold War anxieties, inherited American ideals, similar religious and moral heritages, and a burgeoning economy that provided most people with at least the hope of sharing in the American dream. In such a setting, pragmatism could draw on shared moral capital and act both as an effective broker and as a moderating influence that could help build further consensus, despite calls for individualism and despite the many deep cultural and ideological differences that lurked beneath the surface.

Once those differences surfaced in the next decades, pragmatism remained the mainstay of moderate liberals, particularly in politics, where the art of compromise had long been recognized as the key to success. There is a good argument, furthermore, that in a highly diverse society where there is no way to settle on first principles, pragmatism as the basis for a public philosophy is preferable to any truly ideological alternative in which the ideals of a minority would be imposed on everyone else. Even granting that argument, however, it is not hard to see why the heirs to moderate-liberal pragmatism of recent decades so often look ineffectual. Theirs may be the best approach, compared to more rigid alternatives. Yet it is an approach that is inherently weak when it comes to taking stands on first principles. Even when it was in its prime, as in the consensus era of the 1950s, pragmatism was dependent on shared moral capital. The problem since then is that the less there is of such shared capital, the less effective the pragmatist tradition appears.

The midcentury emphases on individual autonomy and nonconformity also tended to weaken the nation's resources for cultivating moral capital. Traditionally those resources had been cultivated by subcommunities, often ethnic and/or religious in nature, that provided some grounding in a moral tradition and in mores that encouraged community loyalties and responsible citizenship. Yet one of the implications that might be drawn from the celebration of autonomy was that one should leave the petty constraints of one's community of origin, and become a law unto oneself.

Recognizing this weakness in the moderate-liberal pragmatist tradition, which may be a weakness inherent to modernized, secular, non-ideologically driven, widely diverse societies, helps us to better understand why the promise of restoring firmly based first principles would seem so attractive, particularly to people with traditional religious sensibilities.

THE 1950s WAS AN ERA when Protestant Christianity still held a respected, even if mostly honorary, place in American public life, and part of the appeal for fundamentalistic (or militantly conservative) evangelical Protestants in the late 1970s to organize as a major political movement had to do with restoring that respect. The irony, of course, was that the mainstream public Protestantism of the 1950s was broad and often mixed with "the Judeo-Christian heritage," and hence it was just the sort of liberal religion that revivalist Protestants typically denounced. Yet, at that same time, fundamentalists and other revivalist Protestants were enthusiastic about generalized religion in politics when it appeared in the form of civil religion. They were pleased that many political leaders routinely and with evident sincerity invoked Americans' shared faith in God as what most separated them from communism. And they were also happy that Bible reading and prayers were still mandated in many public schools and that Christian invocations were commonplace at public events, even if they thought these should be taken more seriously. So, for conservative evangelical Protestants two decades later, one of the attractions of joining in a national political movement was the promise to restore public acknowledgment that America had a Christian base.

This rapid transition—the transition from being avowed outsiders during the 1950s to proclaiming themselves, by the late 1970s, the "Moral Majority," as well as true American insiders who should have cultural dominance—was possible because of a deep ambivalence in the American fundamentalist-evangelical heritage. On the one hand, conservative evangelicals were heirs to twentieth-century fundamentalism, which often involved militantly separatist reactions against mainstream American religion and culture. They set up their own separatist denominations, Bible churches, parachurch ministries, and Bible colleges; insisted on strict mores that would distinguish them from unbelievers; and were premillennialists, disparaging social and political solutions as they waited for Christ's return. Yet, on the other hand, they were heirs also to an even more deeply rooted American evangelical heritage that went back to the nineteenth century, when Protestant dominance was taken for granted. In some regions of the country, especially the South, revivalist Protestants still enjoyed that sense of cultural ownership. Furthermore, almost no matter how separatist and ardently premillennialist the fundamentalists and other conservative evangelicals became, they had remained fervently patriotic and anti-Communist. That part of their insider heritage continued intact. Hence, they were shaped by the patriotism of World War II and the Cold War at least as much as other Americans were. So, in the 1970s, when conservative evangelicals called for "taking back" America, they were tacitly calling for a return to a time when such strongly anti-Communist patriotism had been more widely shared, in the 1950s. They were also drawing on an older white evangelical sense of cultural guardianship, or an informal "Christian" establishment, that they were proposing to restore.

Conservative religious people often felt most keenly a desire to restore the public standards of the 1950s in the area of family values and sexuality. Before the religious right coalesced as a political movement, many of its constituents had already been alarmed by the sexual revolution of the 1960s. In part, their reactions involved direct revulsion against the permissiveness of the counterculture, but they also saw modern psychology and its celebration of individualistic self-expression as a source of the breakdown of traditional standards. Conservative evangelicals had been exploring alternative psychologies for some time, and radical, "biblically based" psychological theories as alternatives to secular outlooks had wide appeal. For instance, Tim LaHaye, later a leading figure in the political right, first rose to fame as the author of a pop-psychology volume, *The Spirit-Controlled Temperament* (1966), which sold in the millions. Even more influential was the work of Dr. James Dobson, a trained psychologist, who published a parenting book, *Dare to Discipline*, in 1970. That book also sold in the millions. One of Dobson's targets was Dr. Benjamin Spock, whom Dobson saw as having contributed to the breakdown of strict discipline of children and so having helped to foster the undisciplined and morally lax young people of the counterculture. Dobson went on to found the organization Focus on the Family in 1977, and as an author and radio host he became the nation's leading advocate for strict traditional family values, as opposed especially to the agendas of gays and feminists. Dobson attempted to avoid direct political organization, but through the Family Research Council, founded in 1979, he became a leading lobbyist, and he long remained one of the most influential voices of the political right. Even more than forty years later he was implicitly invoking the 1950s by reminding audiences of the damage that the 1960s had done to American sexual morality.[3]

But how did this alarm over cultural changes become transformed into a *political* movement? One major factor was the reaction in conservative religious circles to the role of the national government in promoting the secularizing and permissive trends that were under way. The US Supreme Court decisions of 1962 and 1963 banning mandated prayers in public schools were early fire bells that would long echo as warnings that the government was turning away from religion. Those decisions were in fact part of a larger effort by the Court not only to end Protestant privilege, but also to limit governmental promotion even of "religion-in-general." The Court, moreover, seemed to condone permissiveness when, during the next decade, it came to accept that sexually explicit materials had First Amendment protections as free speech. The contrast between what was permitted and even commonplace by the late 1960s compared to the 1950s was dramatic. In the long run, the 1973 ruling in *Roe v. Wade* legalizing abortion was especially momentous. At first, by far the strongest opposition to *Roe* came from conservative Roman Catholics. For the first several years, fundamentalist and evangelical Protestants did not respond with any great outcry, since abortion had not been one of their traditional concerns. Nonetheless, they did see the decision as part of a larger disturbing permissive trend regarding sexuality. Within the span of little more than a decade, the government had abandoned any role in being an ally of the churches in regulating sexual mores. In the name of pluralism, and reflecting the trend of the time to maximize individual free choice, it seemed to be condoning the sexual revolution.

Not only was the government stepping away from its traditional role in regulating sexual behavior, it was actively promoting the rapidly developing revolution in women's rights, gender equality, homosexuality, and definitions of the family. In 1972, Congress passed the Equal Rights Amendment. Although the amendment seemed simply to guarantee nondiscrimination for women, conservative Christians came to see it as having ominous implications in that it would advance feminist agendas. Phyllis Schlafly, a Roman Catholic, led a strenuous and ultimately successful campaign to prevent ratification of the amendment in a sufficient number of states. Her efforts during the mid-1970s were instrumental in forging a coalition among conservative Catholics and conservative Protestant evangelicals that continued to grow.

Into the mid-1970s conservative Catholics were more active than conservative evangelical Protestants in organizing what would eventually become a larger political coalition. The story of the transition of the American Catholicism of the 1950s to that of the 1980s is both dramatic and complex. Broadly speaking, the Catholic community became divided between, on the one hand, the more liberal elements, which were eager to put the days of authoritarian Catholic ghettoes behind them and assimilate with the American mainstream, and, on the other hand, the more conservative Catholics, who were alarmed by mainstream cultural trends and eager to preserve a strong Catholic identity and the essentials of church teaching, especially regarding marriage and sexuality. Conservative Catholics had a relationship to the early American heritage that was very different from that of most evangelical Protestants. Early "Christian" America had often been anti-Catholic. In the 1950s, anti-Catholicism was still strong, but, simply because of the sheer numbers of Catholics, the church could command some deference. By the 1980s, conservative Catholics had an acute sense of how much that deference had slipped, especially regarding film censorship, birth control, and abortion. Catholics also had a sophisticated heritage of church teaching regarding natural law and the establishment of church teachings in societies. And, after the moderating reforms of Vatican II, these teachings could be adapted to the late twentieth-century American scene in ways that dovetailed with evangelical concerns to restore Christian influences.

DESPITE THESE IMPORTANT Catholic contributions, the religious right would not have had anything like the grassroots impact that it did without the leadership of fundamentalistic Protestants in mobilizing a large segment of revivalist Protestantism as a self-consciously political force.

As late as 1976, the political sensibilities of revivalist evangelicals were still unformed when many of them voted Democratic for Jimmy Carter, largely on the basis that he had declared himself "born again." Prior to 1976, "born again" was not a familiar phrase in mainstream public discourse. Moreover, the term "evangelical" was seldom used, at least not in connection to politics. When *Newsweek* declared 1976 to be "The Year of the Evangelical," the publicity helped to create a sense of potential among evangelicals, who began to think of themselves as a political force. Conservative evangelical and Catholic leaders, however, soon became disillusioned with President Carter. He supported the Equal Rights Amendment, he did not take a stand against abortion, and he was friendly to the Democratic Party agenda to guarantee rights for homosexuals and to broaden the definition of the family. In that context, in 1979 fundamentalist Jerry Falwell founded the Moral Majority, a political-action organization to mobilize religious conservatives. Revivalist evangelicalism had suddenly emerged as a conspicuous player in national politics.

The government was not, of course, the only force in furthering the sexual revolution. Rather, the courts and governmental agencies were responding to much larger social trends and agendas that were energized by vigorous movements and lobbies and supported by most of the media and the intellectual community. The mainstream media and commercial interests often supported the new permissiveness. Nonetheless, for those alarmed by the sexual revolution, the government's role in permitting and promoting it was sufficient to provoke a political response, even among evangelicals who traditionally had warned against political involvements.

One of the factors evident in the support for Ronald Reagan in 1980 was nostalgia for the 1950s. Many conservative Americans had been alarmed by the cultural changes unleashed by the counterculture and antiwar movements of the 1960s and felt that something essential about the culture was fast slipping away. Reagan himself cultivated his image as a champion of traditional values. Just one of many examples was a "Morning

in America" series of TV ads in his 1984 campaign depicting the small-town America of more peaceful and ordered
days.[4] Unquestionably, Reagan's staunch anticommunism also
evoked an image of the 1950s, a time when Americans were
proud to be united by their flag-waving patriotism. Newly politicized revivalist evangelicals were no doubt attracted by this
nostalgia, as were many other Republican voters, but they
added their own variation on the theme. They were not simply
proposing to bring America back to a time when traditional
family values, respect for authority, and unquestioning love
of nation were intact. Rather, they were blending such Rea-
ganesque images with something more basic: America, they
said, needed to return to its "Christian foundations." And understanding what revivalist evangelicals had in mind by such
rhetoric is one key to understanding the cultural wars and revivalist evangelicalism's part in them.

THE FORMULATIONS OF Francis Schaeffer, the most influential theorist of the evangelical side of the religious right, offer an illuminating window into some of the issues involved.
Schaeffer was an American evangelist who spent most of his
career ministering to young people at his chalet, called L'Abri,
in Switzerland. During the late 1960s he became famous in
American evangelical circles for a series of small popular
books that provided critiques of Western cultural trends, arguing that Christianity was the only viable alternative to the
emptiness and the relativism of modern thought. He was also
an important influence in convincing many younger fundamentalists and evangelicals to engage with the arts, literature,

and philosophy. In these early cultural analyses, he almost never mentioned politics, past or present. That changed dramatically in the mid-1970s. Not long after *Roe v. Wade*, while Schaeffer and his son Frank were working on a film series of his cultural critique, Frank argued that they should highlight abortion on demand as evidence of how America had gone wrong. At first the elder Schaeffer strongly resisted this suggestion, on the grounds that abortion was seen mostly as a "Catholic issue" and that he did not want to get into politics. He eventually changed his mind and decided to include it. A critique of the abortion decision became the culminating feature of the series, called *How Should We Then Live?* and the accompanying book by the same title. He and Frank also made the abortion issue the centerpiece of a second series that they developed with Dr. C. Everett Koop (later US surgeon general under Ronald Reagan), called *Whatever Happened to the Human Race?*[5]

In addition to being a major force in raising consciousness among fundamentalists and many other evangelicals regarding the necessity of opposing legalized abortion, Schaeffer provided what became the most influential analyses of what he believed was the larger issue at the heart of the new culture wars. The choice for America, he proclaimed, was simply between a return to Christianity or a takeover by secular humanism and eventually authoritarianism. In *How Should We Then Live?* he wrote that humanists were determined to destroy Christianity and hence they would leave the culture with no adequate basis on which to maintain its values. But, he declared, "society cannot stand chaos." Echoing Erich Fromm's classic account of totalitarianism, Schaeffer continued: "Some group or person will fill the vacuum. An elite will offer us arbitrary absolutes and who will stand in its way?" Schaeffer intimated that this takeover could involve some cooperation with international movements, but he put most of his emphasis on the role of secular humanists in America itself. That formula quickly took root among American fundamentalists. Simple dichotomized choices were the stock in trade of fundamentalists, and Schaeffer, who had fundamentalist roots, was a master at dichotomizing. Moral Majority founder Jerry Falwell often repeated the Christianity-versus-secular-humanism formula, and Tim LaHaye elaborated on it in his very popular 1980 book *The Battle for the Mind*.[6]

Schaeffer himself developed the theme in his most influential call to action, *A Christian Manifesto*, a 1981 book that Falwell described as "probably the most important piece of literature in America today." As in his other recent works, Schaeffer stressed the inevitability of an authoritarian takeover if Bible-believing Christians remained indifferent to politics and failed to take a stand. He believed that the election of Ronald Reagan in 1980 might represent a window of opportunity to reassert Christian values. But he also warned that the power of relativistic secular humanism was so strong in the government, in the courts, and in the schools that it soon might be necessary for Christians to resist through civil disobedience— and even with violence—much as the United States had resisted British tyranny at the time of the American Revolution. Christianity and secular humanism, he emphasized, were opposites. "These two world views stand as totals in complete antithesis to each other," he declared. "It is not too strong to say that we are at war, and there are no neutral parties in the struggle."[7]

Part of Schaeffer's appeal was that he repeatedly reminded his audiences that the loss of what he called America's "Christian consensus" had taken place only within living memory. "It is a horrible thing," he wrote in his final book, *The Great Evangelical Disaster*, published in 1984, "for a man like myself to see my country and my culture go down the drain in my lifetime." He remembered a time when the Christian consensus still prevailed. By a "Christian consensus," he did not mean that everybody was Christian, but rather, that "the Christian worldview, and biblical knowledge in particular, were widely disseminated throughout the culture and were a decisive influence in giving shape to the culture." Such outlooks were characteristic, he said, of "Reformation countries and in our own country until the last forty to sixty years," when "most people believed these things—albeit sometimes only in a vague way." Schaeffer's audiences, at least in many regions of the country, especially across the South and in some areas of the Midwest, may have recalled the 1950s as the sort of time he was evoking, when evangelical Christianity was virtually the default religion. Schaeffer himself was from the Northeast, where the changes had come earlier; in the 1950s, he had already been a separatist fundamentalist attacking the mainstream culture and its churches. So he set the date of the end of the Christian consensus further back, to the 1930s.[8]

Schaeffer combined nostalgia for more Christian-friendly times with his own version of an argument that was reemerging in popularity among fundamentalistic evangelicals around the bicentennial year of 1976: that America had been founded as a Christian nation. Schaeffer emphasized that the American nation was based on a Christian consensus inherited specifically from the Reformation. He argued that the principles on which the United States was founded, especially the idea that higher law applied even to kings, came from Scottish Protestantism at the time of the English Civil Wars of the mid-1600s. Even though Schaeffer acknowledged that most of the American founders were not born-again Christians, and that they had their blind spots (as regarding slavery), he nonetheless insisted that they still operated on the Reformation "Christian base." Those principles, he believed, dominated American culture until recent decades. Secular humanism was destroying those principles and would inevitably lead to total relativism, chaos, and then totalitarianism. To remain neutral, as so many fundamentalist and evangelical Christians had tried to do at midcentury, would be to capitulate to government enforcement of a worldview that was the opposite of Christianity. As Schaeffer put it, "Here is a sentence to memorize: '*To make no decision in regard to the growth of authoritarian government is already a decision for it.*'"[9]

Francis Schaeffer, of course, does not represent the whole of the religious right—he had, for instance, little connection with the important conservative Catholic part of the movement—but his outlook serves to illustrate some significant dimensions of the fundamentalistic evangelical wing of that movement. Viewed in relation to the mainstream American outlooks of the 1950s, one feature of the movement was its strong reaction against pragmatic liberalism, which it now understood in Schaeffer's framework as part of the "secular humanism" that had led to the moral relativism evident in America since the late 1960s. Schaeffer added the motif, reminiscent of Erich Fromm, that if a society lost its moral moorings, totalitarianism would fill the vacuum. So pragmatic liberalism, which to its proponents in the 1950s seemed the best defense against ideological extremes, now could be seen as opening the door to totalitarianism. Even if Communists were rare on the home front in the 1980s, secular humanists were everywhere, and only a stance of cultural warfare could stop their destruction of American liberties. Schaeffer repeatedly called for reestablishing a Christian consensus, but ironically, "consensus" had become a fighting word. He depicted the cultural crises in the most urgent terms as he issued calls to arms. So he wrote in 1982 with typical hyperbole in a foreword to his associate John Whitehead's *The Second American Revolution*, "If there is still an entity known as 'the Christian church' by the end of the century, operating with any semblance of liberty . . . it will probably have John Whitehead and his book to thank." The book, he went on, "lays the foundation and framework for fighting the tyrannical, secularist, humanistic power." Like the early American patriots, Christians would have to be ready to fight for their liberties. Restoring America's "Christian base" would require enlisting in America's culture wars.[10]

Granting that there were and are many highly significant issues involved in these political concerns that deserve consideration on their merits, it is also important to recognize that once the matters are framed in terms of warfare and simple either-or choices it becomes virtually impossible to negotiate those issues in a pluralistic society. That is especially the case when the issues are framed in terms of returning America to its Christian roots, as is standard fare in the outlooks of the fundamentalist-evangelical political right. Partly the problem is rhetorical. Typically, evangelicals speak of their views as shaped by "the Bible alone." The more fundamentalistic or militant they are, the more they divide reality into simple dichotomies, such as "Christian" and "non-Christian." That leaves little room for making other distinctions. So when they talk about reinstituting America's Christian basis, it sounds as though they are proposing a return to something like the early New England Puritan order of the 1600s, when the government was based on explicitly biblical principles, and discrimination against non-Christians was taken for granted.

Even though the rhetoric sounds authoritarian, as though the nation would be redefined as exclusively Christian and its law would be based on the Bible, the vast majority of fundamentalists and evangelicals of the religious right were—and are—in fact committed to religious liberty. Many are Baptists, whose forebears were in the forefront of the campaign for religious freedom at the time of the American Revolution. More broadly, despite their exclusive-sounding "Christian" rhetoric, they are also deeply committed to the principles embodied in the nation's founding documents. They are heirs to the synthesis of Protestant and more secular principles that were characteristic of what is here being called the American enlightenment.[11] Once again, they need to be understood as deeply ambivalent toward the American heritage. On the one hand, they often speak as prophetic outsiders proclaiming that the nation is under judgment for its many failings. On the other hand, they also speak as the true insiders who are preserving an eighteenth-century national heritage that was essentially "Christian."

Fundamentalists and evangelicals of the religious right often have difficulty recognizing their own mix of biblical and more secular principles because they typically use only two categories in their analyses: Christian and non-Christian. That limitation can be best illustrated in the outpouring of books in recent decades claiming to prove that the founding fathers were Christians. In their own ministries, the authors of these books insist that only the "born again" will enter the kingdom of heaven. Yet when it comes to the nation's founders, most of whom were not orthodox evangelical Christians, these very conservative biblicists end up endorsing a remarkably broad definition of "Christian." Perhaps the most telling of the many examples that could be cited is that in 2012, David Barton, the most popular and influential writer on America's Christian origins, published a book celebrating Thomas Jefferson's faith. The fact of the matter is that Jefferson was openly and sometimes militantly anti-orthodox and anti-evangelical. During the election of 1800, many orthodox Protestants strongly opposed him for his unconventional religious views. Barton's zeal to claim Jefferson as a Christian believer led to so many distortions that, when these were documented, his publisher, Thomas Nelson, ceased publication.[12]

Francis Schaeffer, who recognized the unorthodoxy of most of the founders, tried to solve the problem by attributing their views regarding rights and freedom to the Reformation. In fact, though, the early Protestant governments of the Reformation period were not concerned about protecting liberties in the same way that the founders later were in the American republic. Those ideals developed in the British enlightenment in the seventeenth and eighteenth centuries. They did have a discernibly Protestant lineage, such as in concerns about the sanctity of conscience, but the founders' ideals were also shaped by factors beyond the Protestant principle of "the Bible alone." These influences included classical political principles, classical and Christian natural-law traditions, modern scientific empiricism, the growing trust in the authority of common rationality, emerging ideals that individuals should be self-determining, and practical self-interested concern regarding political and economic freedoms. It is one thing to say that some versions of the resulting mix were "Christian," in the sense of being compatible with biblical or church teachings. Yet, historically speaking, the actual mix was far from being simply Christian or Protestant, even if it included significant Christian elements.

The complex heritage of the evangelical religious right, as shaped, among other things, both by biblicist born-again revivalism and broader principles developed during the eighteenth-century American enlightenment, helps to explain some of its paradoxes, apparent contradictions, and blind spots. The biblicist side is often absolutist and militant, invoking stark choices between serving the Lord of Hosts or the Baal of secular humanism. The enlightenment heritage allows militantly conservative fundamentalists to in fact affiliate with the wide coalition represented in the Republican Party and to participate in the give-and-take of practical politics, despite all the compromises that inevitably requires. In the strict biblicist view, the American nation can be seen as having forfeited any claim to God's blessings and as being under judgment for its open sins, so that the only hope is to trust in Jesus to return to set things right. But the enlightenment heritage tells the evangelical religious right that the American principles of civil freedom, self-determination, and free enterprise are the bcst there are, and that evangelicals can therefore unreservedly embrace the American civil religion and condemn anyone who questions that America has a special place in God's plan. The strictly biblicist heritage fosters a rhetoric that sounds theocratic and culturally imperialist, and in which a Christian consensus would seem to allow little room for secularists or their rights. The enlightenment heritage means that the leading motif in their politics is the necessity of protecting freedoms, especially the personal and economic freedoms of the classically liberal tradition. So when members of the evangelical religious right speaks about returning to a "Christian" America, they may sound as though they would return to days of the early Puritans; yet, practically speaking, the ideal they are invoking is tempered by the American enlightenment and is reminiscent of the days of the informal Protestant establishment, when Christianity was respected, but most of the culture operated on more secular terms.

Even though the populist religious right is marked by paradoxical features, it should also be given credit for drawing attention to important questions about the role of religion in

American public life. After the decline of the mainline Protestant establishment, the society was left with no real provision as to how religious viewpoints would be represented in the public sphere, such as in politics or education. At the same time, an immense revolution in mores had been accelerated by the upheavals of the late 1960s. Many prevailing moral standards promoted in popular culture, in commercial culture, by the government, and in public education were at odds with the traditional religious teachings not only of conservative Protestants but also of many of the other traditionalist religious groups across the country. An important question was how such conservative religious viewpoints, which were largely minority viewpoints, might be represented and protected in the public domain. Advocates of the religious right were rightly concerned to guard their own freedoms of religious expression and action. Yet they seldom had a theory of how to do the same unto others as they would have done unto themselves— that is, they rarely spoke of how to provide equal protection for religious and secular viewpoints with which they did not agree.[13]

Toward a More Inclusive Pluralism

Popular fundamentalist and conservative evangelical leaders who speak of returning to a Christian America are not alone in their failure to address questions of how to deal with both religious and secular diversity in public life. The mainstream secular culture of the past half-century, despite its concerns for justice regarding other sorts of diversity (such as racial, ethnic, or sexual diversity), has not yet effectively addressed the difficult question of religious diversity. One way to understand that neglect is as an inheritance of the way that the mainstream liberal-moderate secular and religious culture dealt with such matters in the 1950s. An account of the characteristic midcentury outlooks and their legacy can help us today in thinking about alternative approaches for the future.

Despite the prestige of mainline Protestantism in the 1950s, and despite all the public expressions of a broad piety, some of the most prominent and pervasive ideals of the mainstream culture were in deep conflict with the traditionalist sorts of religious faith held by many Americans. To return to a theme mentioned before in other contexts: one of the major implications of the midcentury consensus critiques of conformity and affirmations of scientific outlooks and individual autonomy was that they seemed to promise a new moral order that would help to free individuals from traditional communities and moral strictures. Much of the religious revival was fostered in a myriad of traditionally religious communities—Catholic, fundamentalist, Pentecostal, holiness, Jewish, Eastern Orthodox, African American, Midwest Lutheran, Southern Baptist, and many more. Yet the message that one would most often hear from the cultural mainstream—as in the national media, public education, and academia—was that one would be better off as an individual liberated from such community constraints. Individual self-development and self-fulfillment should be one's overriding goals.

That often subtle message—that it was better to trust yourself than to follow subcommunities or their traditions—was symptomatic of the way that midcentury mainstream consensus-minded culture most often dealt with diversity and pluralism. A chorus of voices, including the more progressive mainline Protestant leadership, affirmed a flexible, inclusive pluralism as one of the great virtues of mainstream American life. At midcentury, American society still had a long way to go before it was truly inclusive, but the ideal was at least in place that openness and tolerance were essential to a healthy, thriving society. To be truly "pluralistic" meant to be open-minded rather than sectarian and dogmatic. That was especially the message of the more secular liberal thinkers. When, for instance, Arthur Schlesinger Jr. dismissed Walter Lippmann's advocacy of a return to natural law, it was on the grounds that the pundit was forgetting "the reality of pluralism." Intellectually, to be pluralistic meant that one should be empirical and pragmatic, following the evidence wherever it led, rather than being guided by preconceptions. When David Riesman, for instance, wrote of *The Lonely Crowd* in his 1961 preface that it "was one of a number of books which in recent years have eschewed dogmatism and fanaticism and preferred openness, pluralism, and empiricism," he was simply summarizing the consensus liberal ideals of the day. These were ideals held not only by scholars; they were also becoming widely prevalent in business, politics, the media, and everyday life.[1]

An important feature of this outlook was that it took for granted a progressive and cumulative model of truth. It assumed that, ideally, the human race progressed by accumulating new insights and discoveries that proved valuable for collective human flourishing. Because impositions of irrational ideologies or dogmas could inhibit or even destroy this growth, a society needed to cultivate the qualities of being empirical, open-minded, and inclusive. Disinterested scientific methodology provided one valuable model, and accumulated scientific knowledge was the surest way to weed out folk beliefs and other nonsense. Although this version of inclusive pluralism allowed room for considerable varieties of experiences and outlooks, such as religious or imaginative ones, that went beyond what science might teach, it also took for granted that educated people should test their beliefs against shared, accumulated, scientifically based knowledge. Such empirically tested beliefs and practices would provide the best hope for building consensus and promoting collective intellectual and social progress. Though people would inevitably disagree on particulars, they would have a shared foundation for agreement as to basics. That had been "the noble dream" of progressive-minded people since the eighteenth century. Even if the philosophical foundations for such hopes were admittedly more flexible, or perhaps more shaky, than in the days of enlightenment confidence, the assumptions regarding shared, scientifically tested outlooks still held out hope for social progress.[2]

Thomas Kuhn, a Berkeley historian of science, would in 1962 publish his groundbreaking book *The Structure of Scientific Revolutions*, which would help to undermine the remaining foundations for these progressive cumulative views of truth. In the context of the radical pluralism of the later 1960s, Kuhn's book would emerge as one of the most influential American texts of the twentieth century. Kuhn argued that even natural science itself was not a cumulative enterprise built on a foundation of objective starting points. Instead, it was shaped by "paradigms," or fundamental assumptions about reality. These paradigms could undergo revolutionary changes, such as in the Copernican revolution, when scientists replaced the assumption that earth was a fixed place with the model that everything was in motion. Such paradigm shifts made the seemingly objective science of one era incommensurable with the seemingly objective science of the next era. Eventually, the term "paradigm shift" would become commonplace in American thought, and the idea of objective social authority based on scientific models would be widely questioned. But in the 1950s, almost everyone was working within the old paradigm, in which it was assumed that natural scientific methodologies did provide more or less objective foundations so far as they went and hence could provide essential common components in building cultural consensus.[3]

So the idea of progress was still alive at midcentury. Most commentators took for granted that, generally speaking, the best ideas were recent inventions. Faith in progress had become somewhat chastened since World War I, but the assumption that newer, superior ideas were steadily replacing older, inferior ones—C. S. Lewis at the time called it "chronological snobbery"—still was characteristic of the era. Such assumptions, even if sometimes tempered, were particularly strong regarding views that purported to have the authority of science on their side. That included fields such as psychology and sociology that offered the latest insights on human nature and behavior. It was not uncommon to speak as though people should bring their views up to date with the latest scientifically based findings in such areas, much as they might need to keep up with the latest technology. Even though the sciences often led to disagreements, and even though one had to be pluralistic in the sense of allowing for differences among various modern schools of thought, empirically tested views could provide the basis for an evolving consensus of opinion among right-thinking people.[4]

The most striking example of such assumptions of progress and normativity was the assumption that parochial traditional religious views would eventually die out as civilization and education advanced. Scholars typically took for granted "the secularization thesis," which said that as modernity advanced, traditional religions would decline. Ethnoreligious communities and Bible-belt religion were assumed to be on the way out. The frenzied activities of groups such as Pentecostals and fundamentalists, even if they attracted large audiences, could be viewed as the last flaming of a dying culture. Many factors—such as industrialization, urbanization, mobility, and new technologies—were contributing, ushering in an essentially secular age. Amid these other forces, modern scientific outlooks could help people become autonomous individuals. People were taught that they should adopt a new, scientifically informed ethic of constructive self-realization and self-determination as they freed themselves from the restraints of their parochial origins.

Such assumptions, together with accompanying ideals of inclusive pluralism shaping a progressive consensus, left mainstream American culture with little concern for incorporating real religious diversity into its public life. If traditional religious voices were backward and dying out, there was no need to develop a rationale for incorporating them into mainstream discussions in the sophisticated media or academia. Efforts to cultivate and preserve a place for religion in public life concentrated instead largely on religious views that were themselves up-to-date and progressive, such as those of liberal Protestantism.

By the 1980s, mainline Protestant voices, although still present, had lost much of the prestige they had enjoyed at midcentury. In addition, the symbolic privileges of broadly Protestant Christianity had been reduced, as they were in, most famously, the Supreme Court rulings of the 1960s banning mandated Christian exercises in public schools. Mainline Protestantism also voluntarily stepped away from some of its privileged status. Many church-affiliated colleges and universities, for instance, greatly reduced the presence of their own denominational heritages and cultivated a diversity of voices similar to that found in the rest of academia.

So, with the voices thus muted of the group that traditionally had most effectively represented religious interests in public life, the prevailing outlook became that the public domain—whether in education, politics, or public discourse—ought to aim at operating without reference to specific religious viewpoints. The most common means to promote such neutrality was by way of more consistent privatization of religious belief. That approach had considerable appeal. All religious views could be treated equally. They could be respected as personal choices, so long as they did not get in the way of the public business of society. This view was often expressed in a metaphor taken from Jefferson, that of a "wall of separation" between church and state. The Supreme Court had invoked this image as early as 1947, and it was used again in the 1960s as a basis for ending prayer in public schools. It also became popular shorthand in the moderate-liberal mainstream for thinking about relationships between religion and the public sphere.

The great problem with the "wall of separation" metaphor was, as the courts came to recognize, that it proved to be impossible to draw any consistent line between the secular public sphere and the religion of the private sphere. A sizable minority of Americans was seriously religious, and their religious beliefs had inevitable influences on their activities in the public domain, whether in politics, business, or education. It is one thing to try to draw a line between "church and state," two sorts of institutions. But no consistent line of separation can even be imagined between the far larger entities of "religion and society." Religion is seldom a strictly spiritual matter; rather, it involves moral prescriptions as to how to act in everyday secular affairs. Although religious people may reasonably be expected to act with a degree of civility in the public domain, showing respect for others and their differing views, it is not reasonable or practical to expect them to act in the public realm without reference to their deeply held, religiously based moral convictions. So, even if privatization has proven valuable as a way of encouraging social harmony up to a point, it is a principle that cannot address the question of equity in the public sphere in dealing with inevitable differences based on religious conviction.[5]

Mainstream American culture has never had a fully adequate way of dealing equitably with religious diversity in the public domain. On the positive side, one of the great achievements of the new nation was that religious toleration was instituted from the beginning. What was missing (and understandably so, in that era of religious establishments, when Protestants were in the vast majority) was a principle for moving beyond mere toleration. Rather, Protestants understandably protected their own influence and interests, but they also worked to keep other faiths out of the public domain, as their long record of militant anti-Catholicism and anti-Mormonism illustrates. Even so, because America was a democracy, Catholics and Mormons could gain some political power, and thus some influence in the public domain, despite Protestant efforts to the contrary. When the mainline Protestant establishment did become more tolerant, in the mid-twentieth century, it was in the form of a tri-faith (Protestant-Catholic-Jew) inclusive pluralism. That sort of inclusivism, based in liberal religion, failed to include fundamentalists, Pentecostals, and other conservative evangelicals as well as Mormons, Orthodox Jews, conservative Catholics, Muslims, Hindus, and many others who did not fit the mainline religious profile.[6]

The major historical alternative to Protestant dominance and privilege was a more secular approach that made privatization the ideal. That seemed to be the implication of Jefferson's "wall of separation," a position shared by some Baptists, who had histories of opposing religious establishments. It became the favored view of secularists in the twentieth century. It offered, as has just been observed, no theory for dealing with inevitable expressions of religious diversity in the public domain. Secularists and academics generally, who had made recognition of other sorts of diversity one of the great causes of the 1960s and 1970s, were seldom interested in religion. Race, class, and gender were the new categories of the present, while religion, they typically thought, was a fading category from the past. They still took the secularization thesis for granted, much as their predecessors had in the 1950s.[7]

In the meantime, however, a funny thing was happening on the way to the secularization of American life: traditionalist religious subcommunities were not going away, but often were growing in strength. Some, such as older ethnic urban Roman Catholic communities, did suffer attrition as parishioners moved to the suburbs, and many cradle Catholics, having adopted ideals of American autonomy that did not fit well with church authority, simply stopped attending. But other new Catholic immigrant groups, especially Latino Catholics, took their places. More open immigration policies fostered other varieties of ethnoreligious communities, many of which were non-Christian and non-Western. In addition, New Age sensibilities generated new kinds of spirituality and revived old ones. Perhaps most remarkably, the more conservative revivalist Protestant groups were thriving rather than diminishing.

With American religious practice not actually diminishing, and with religious diversity growing, a new challenge was emerging. Simply including progressive consensus religious voices in the mainstream on the 1950s model was not feasible. Neither was it possible to establish a consistent privatization. So here was the challenge: How, in an era when diversity was being celebrated in other respects, might it be possible to construct a mainstream discourse that recognized roles for a variety of *religious* voices? And this is still the question today.

When the religious right emerged as an organized political movement in the late 1970s, it, too, as has been recounted, lacked attention to the question of how to ensure equity for widely diverse voices in the public domain. Even though militantly conservative Christians had not been part of the liberal Protestant establishment of the 1950s, their instinct was to propose a return to something that would look a lot like it, but with conservatives such as themselves in charge of defining the cultural consensus. The religious right could encompass some internal religious diversity, since it included culturally conservative Catholics, Mormons, Orthodox Jews, and others. Yet what it glaringly lacked, especially in the popular Protestant zeal to return America to its alleged Christian roots, were accounts of how such a proposed restoration would deal with greater diversity, either religious or secular. Militantly conservative Protestants, just getting over their belligerent anti-Catholicism, did not have a heritage of thinking about such issues beyond the Baptist principle of separation of church and state. They now spoke of "secular humanists" as though they were the enemy to be excluded in a Christianized America. Conservative Roman Catholics had a religious heritage in which, until recently, it had been held that, ideally, Catholicism should be the state religion. That meant that Catholics were only just beginning to address questions of how to deal equitably with religious and cultural diversity. Some serious conservative theorists, both Catholic and Protestant, did indeed provide some valuable engagement with those issues. But in the more popular manifestations of the religious right, their nuanced voices were often drowned out by strident and simplistic calls for a return to America's original Christian consensus.[8]

The fact was that the stridency of the religious right's demands for America to return traditionalist Christianity to the cultural mainstream only made most other parties less in-clined to address issues of religious equity. The rhetoric of the religious right about "taking back" America and its institu-tions only made it easier for the more secular-minded people to dismiss religion as simply a threat to diversity in the public sphere. Conservative Christian attacks on the feminist and gay agendas reinforced the tendency of the champions of cul-tural inclusivism to favor a more thoroughly secular culture. So even though the value of allowing a diversity of viewpoints to be heard was increasingly being recognized in the cultural mainstream, proponents of diversity were seldom inclined to think about how to include a diversity of religious viewpoints.

So as the era of the culture wars emerged by about 1980, none of the major parties had a well-developed heritage of thinking about how to accommodate religious diversity as it related to the public domain. Even as other sorts of multi-culturalism were reaching the peak of their influence, most Americans lacked any adequate tradition for dealing with deeply held religious differences in the public sphere.

CROSS-CULTURAL COMPARISONS often help people see their own culture in a new light. In this case, the peculiarities of typically American ways of dealing with religious pluralism can be brought into focus by comparing them with an alter-native view that arose in a slightly different cultural context. This alternative view does not resolve all the remarkably com-plex problems regarding religion and culture. But it does offer a starting point or framework for thinking about them that differs from the dominant American models. This outlook was developed in the Netherlands by the Dutch theologian, churchman, political leader, and publicist Abraham Kuyper in the late nineteenth century. Not everything in Kuyper is suited to addressing twenty-first-century American issues. He was a man of his times, and his outlooks were sometimes parochial. They need to be updated if they are to be applied to contemporary settings, as indeed they have been by a number of his current admirers. For understanding the underlying fundamental issues, however, the differences between his starting point and the treatment of the issue in most of the American Protestant heritage are nonetheless instructive.[9]

Abraham Kuyper, who lived from 1837 to 1920, was easily one of the leading modern thinkers regarding religion and culture. He also had, not incidentally, an extraordinarily multifaceted career. Trained as a theologian, he began as pastor in the Reformed Church, which had formerly been the nation's state church. His efforts to reform that denomination led to a division and the founding of a new Reformed denomination. He was also the editor of an influential newspaper as well as a prolific writer. He helped to found a university, and he then taught there as a theologian. And in addition to these ecclesiastical, editorial, academic, and intellectual activities, he also had an impressive political career: he founded a political party that he long headed, was a member of parliament, and served as prime minister of the Netherlands from 1901 to 1905. Kuyper, who was first of all a person of principles, also had the energy and force of will to create reforming institutions that would embody those principles.

Kuyper's principles are illuminating especially because of how they contrast with the dominant American models. His most helpful insights reflect in part the differences between the cultural and intellectual settings of the Netherlands and the United States. Late nineteenth-century America had been indelibly shaped by the Civil War. Because that war had been about preserving the Union, national unification was a dominant theme in the social thought of the era. The two political parties that emerged from the war were "liberal" fraternal twins, both essentially nonideological. Faced with a flood of immigration after the war, the great social challenge was to assimilate peoples with all sorts of differences into this cultural-political mainstream. The Netherlands also was dealing with issues of rising liberalism and national consolidation. It had some heritage of religious diversity, but was relatively stable in its religious and ethnic makeup. In 1848 the Dutch state gave up efforts to regulate religious groups, and the central question for the next generation, as Kuyper saw it, was how to preserve distinctive subcommunities, especially religious subcommunities, in the face of growing secular trends and modern pressures toward uniformity. Owing in no small part to Kuyper's own efforts, the Netherlands, which had a parliamentary system, developed multiple ideologically and religiously defined parties. So, in the Netherlands, unlike in the American two-party setting, enlightenment-based liberalism was only one option among many. Another difference from the typical American outlooks was that Americans tended to think about things in practical ways, from the bottom up, rather than from the top down; Kuyper, by contrast, was working in an intellectual setting dominated by European idealism, in which it was characteristic to look at things holistically from the top down. Kuyper himself adopted a holistic stance, but with principles derived not from modern idealism, but from his Augustinian Reformed heritage, in which God, the creator of all reality, must be the starting point for all understanding.

One especially important feature of Kuyper's outlook is that it illustrates how epistemology, or the study of the nature of knowledge, can help shape social policy. Kuyper's approach literally provides a place to start in rethinking these issues. Most American Protestants regarded science and reason as ideologically neutral, and presented faith as something that went beyond the kind of objective but limited knowledge that science and reason could produce. Kuyper, by way of contrast, worked from a principle enunciated by St. Augustine: "I believe in order to understand." Faith preceded understanding, and so faith informed and shaped understanding. Working from this principle, Kuyper insisted that reason, natural science, and methodological naturalism were not ideologically neutral. Even the most technical of natural sciences, he observed, operated within the framework of the faith, or higher commitments, of the practitioner.[10]

At the purely technical level, people of various faiths (either religious or secular higher commitments) might work side by side and get the same technical results. But as soon as they reflected on the larger implications of their science or their reasoning, they would begin to understand those results in radically different contexts. As an Augustinian Christian, Kuyper developed this principle as it related to differences in the thinking of Christians and non-Christians—that is, of those who by God's grace understood reality through the lens of Christian faith as revealed in Scripture, on the one hand, and of those, on the other hand, who viewed reality through other lenses. Regarding that division, which for Christians is the most fundamental one, Kuyper could say, "there are two kinds of people and two kinds of science." Kuyper used "science" here in the broad sense of any intellectual inquiry.[11]

The significance of things, he insisted, depended on their relationships, and so Christians perceived everything (trees, birds, humans, and even social institutions, the arts, labor, capital, and so on) in relation to their creator, the triune God. Those who did their science and reasoning in the context of recognizing those relationships saw dimensions and implications of things that other people did not apprehend. Reflecting on the relationship of reality to its loving creator would reshape the meaning of even the humblest enterprises. Even though from an Augustinian Christian perspective, the greatest divide was between those who recognized and trusted the triune God of Scripture and those who did not, in fact the human race was divided among peoples of many different highest commitments. So one could say, following Kuyper, that there were many highest commitments that provided frameworks within which differing peoples did their science and other reasoning.[12]

These views are closely related to a conception of pluralism in the public arena that has been characterized as "confessional pluralism" or "principled pluralism." Such pluralism would attempt to take the differences among varieties of both religious and nonreligious perspectives seriously. By way of contrast, in the dominant midcentury American liberal-moderate view of building toward consensus, scientific outlooks were often presented as ideologically neutral. For instance, when the US Supreme Court in the 1960s was ruling against prayer and the promotion of particular religious viewpoints in public schools, it suggested that an impartial alternative would be to teach "objectively" *about* religion. In the Kuyperian approach to pluralism, there is no conceding that modern scientific methods are objective so far as they go and hence could serve as neutral ways to view religious faiths. Rather, the outlook recognizes from the outset that the modern world is divided by fundamental differences in underlying faiths and commitments, some of which have nontheistic naturalism as their starting points and some of which have various forms of theism and openness to the supernatural as their starting points. Hence, societies, especially in their schooling and intellectual lives, but also in their public conversations and debates about morality, justice, and the like, should be built around the recognition that varieties of viewpoints, including varieties of both religious and secular viewpoints, exist and ought to be included in a genuine pluralism. There would be no illusion, as developed in the American case, that a national consensus might be built on an ideologically neutral basis, and that therefore neutral scientific models provided the best hope for finding objective foundations for such a public consensus.[13] In contrast to Kuyper, the mainstreams of American Protestantism from the eighteenth century through the mid-twentieth century shared a tradition of having reconciled their faith to the moderate American enlightenment, so that they rarely offered any critique of the idea that science and reason were, in principle, ideologically neutral. That was true of both theological liberals and conservatives. Reinhold Niebuhr, for instance, was characteristic of the liberal outlook in conceding autonomy to scientific inquiry, so long as it kept to its proper domain of nature and did not intrude into the areas of human freedom. American theological conservatives, in the meantime, had been shaped by enlightenment commonsense philosophy and typically insisted that objective science and reason would support biblical faith. Even when they viewed Darwinian evolution as hostile to Christianity, they typically insisted that they were not against objective natural science, but that truly objective science would support the biblical account.[14]

Abraham Kuyper developed his views explicitly as a critique of the enlightenment ideal of a neutral universal reason, yet he was not a postmodern relativist. Rather than holding that various claims to "truth" were artificial human constructions, he believed that God had created a reality that all people could know, in part if never completely. So he believed there was a place for shared rationality in holding a society together. Even though, as a result of human sinfulness, people were sharply divided as to their first commitments, they were still creatures of God who shared some commonalities in experiencing the same created order. So they also shared some important elements of common rationality and moral sensibilities, such as a sense of justice. Even though differing peoples need to recognize that no one stands on neutral ground, but all are shaped by their highest commitments, they can still go on to look for shared principles on which they can agree as a basis for working together. Kuyper believed that since all people share experience in God's ordered reality, such areas of agreement among peoples of various religious or secular faiths could be considerable. Kuyper often spoke of God's "common grace," by which he meant goods that were extended to all people, such as natural resources, in which all can share, and common institutions for ordering and keeping peace in societies.

Abraham Kuyper combined the ideal of "confessional pluralism" in the public arena with an emphasis on recognizing and respecting a multiplicity of authorities in the structures of society. He saw these structures as reflecting a God-ordained ordering of social reality that people of all sorts of faiths could recognize as beneficial. Governments are one sort of agency of authority, but churches (and other religious groups), families, schools, businesses, agencies of the arts, and so forth are institutions with their own authority, each in its own sphere. The primary function of government is to promote justice and to act as a sort of referee, patrolling the boundaries among the spheres of society, protecting the sovereignty due within each sphere, adjudicating conflicts, and ensuring equal rights and equal protections for confessional groups, so far as that is possible. In this richly pluralistic view, society thrives when it promotes the health and integrity of what more recently have often been called "mediating institutions." Such institutions likewise should stay within their spheres of competence. So, for instance, just as the government does not have competence to rule on confessional matters for churches, so churches and other religious groups should not be aspiring to dictate to the government and to impose their own views on the whole.[15]

Such a conception of pluralism, although developed in a specifically Augustinian framework, would be compatible with many other outlooks and would help provide an alternative to the culture-wars mentality that has plagued American life for the past generation. Clearly, because of its theological premises, updated versions of Kuyperian pluralism would be most useful to Christians. And various sorts of Christians would need to take the lead in providing alternatives to the populist Christian neglect of issues regarding equity and pluralism. For a better understanding of what a Kuyperian outlook might look like today, one could do no better than to start with a 2011 book by Richard Mouw, *Abraham Kuyper: A Short and Personal Introduction*. Or one might explore the website of the Center for Public Justice, which provides examples of "principled pluralism" and suggests readings on its various dimensions. For Christians, especially theologically traditional Christians, the resources are already there for moving beyond culture-wars thinking and the either-or simplicities favored by the American political process. At the same time, although it is unlikely that there will ever be many "atheists for Kuyper," secularists might look at him simply in terms of comparative intellectual history as an alternative to characteristic American assumptions regarding religion and public life. Even though secularists do not share the underlying assumptions of Kuyper's outlook, they might nonetheless share his recog-

nition that faiths (whether secular or religious) shape understanding, his concern for equity, and hence his regard for the
merits of taking religious outlooks seriously in any discussion
of public diversity.

ALTHOUGH THERE MAY BE SIGNS of change, American
society is still caught in the polarized pattern that emerged
in the 1970s and 1980s. At one pole is a liberal culture that
includes most of mainstream academia and entertainment and
that is self-consciously pluralistic in the inclusivist sense, but
is also overwhelmingly secular, so that it does not have much
of a way to deal with religious diversity in public life. At the
other pole is a predominantly religious, conservative, popular
political culture that does not often have a well-thought-out
concept of pluralism that would provide equitable roles for
non-Christian and secularist viewpoints in the public domain.
Partisans of each side regard the other side as essentially imperialistic. Secular liberals believe their freedoms are threatened
by a conservative Christian takeover. Conservative Christians
believe that secularists are excluding their Christian views and
using big government to expand their own dominion. The
fears of each side are exaggerated, but those fears have some
basis in a society that does not have well-developed traditions
or conceptions of pluralism that can embrace a wide range of
both religious and nonreligious viewpoints.

Part of the problem is that Christian conservatives and sec-
ularized liberals each often act as though they see themselves
as the proper heirs to the mid-twentieth-century consensus.
Conservatives view that consensus as more Christian than it

was. Secular liberals today may deny that they advocate any sort of consensus outlook, since they are open to embracing ethnic and racial differences. Yet, when it comes to thinking about religiously based differences, they are likely to sound like midcentury consensus thinkers, who believed that views congenial to secular naturalism were the only ones that should be taken seriously in the public domain. To the extent that they would insist on such a rule, they are in practice asking religious people to assimilate into a melting pot defined by naturalistic intellectual and cultural norms. Each side needs to recognize that neither a religiously based nor a naturalistically based consensus could ever be adequately inclusive.

At the same time that the Kuyperian heritage provides a starting point for thinking about how to take religious differences seriously, its emphasis on common grace also provides a rationale for addressing the troubling issue of how people of fundamentally different outlooks may listen to each other and work together, rather than polarizing around their differences. Politicized American evangelicalism and fundamentalism have rarely addressed this issue well in the past generation. Despite its American enlightenment heritage, which acknowledged a common creator and some shared human common sense, politicized evangelicalism has tended to speak only in terms of dichotomies, as though the only choices were between a fully Christian society and a wholly secular one. A Kuyperian outlook provides a basis for recognizing that there can be both radical differences in fundamental outlooks and also a basis for social and political cooperation, based on the God-given principle of common grace.

SINCE THE 1980S, there has been increasing awareness that religion is not going to go away as a major factor in public life. That reality became widely apparent soon after the fall of the Soviet Union in 1991, when religion, especially Islam, emerged as a leading force in world politics. For Americans, there was no ignoring that reality after the events of 9/11. In the meantime, both Christianity and Islam were growing at remarkable rates in many parts of the world. In the United States, conservative Christianity, rather than fading away, became a major long-term feature of American politics. Some scholars even declared that in the twenty-first century we had entered a "post-secular age."[16] That assessment may prove to be an overstatement—it is hard to tell. One thing is clear, though. It no longer makes sense to maintain, as many of the best observers assumed at midcentury, that secularization is steadily and inevitably advancing, and that religion is receding as the world modernizes. By now there is no denying that the interrelationships among modernity, secularity, and religion are far more complex than that. All three of these may be advancing at the same time.

If we are in an era that can plausibly be called "post-secular," then it is all the more urgent to be thinking carefully about the role of deeply held religious beliefs in the public domain, and about how order and civility can be maintained in society when people of many different "faiths," both religious and secular, are striving to be heard and to have an influence. There is no going back to the 1950s, when a widely shared inclusivist faith was supposed to be a contributing factor in supporting a cultural consensus. Nor does it make sense to go back to, or perhaps perpetuate, the mainstream approach of the 1980s, when many in the liberal cultural establishment viewed varieties of secularism as the only intellectually viable options.

One ideal for a healthy society would be that it sustained diverse, flourishing subcommunities that both retained their own identities and yet also participated in the mainstream public culture. Throughout its history, the United States has had many thriving subcommunities, especially ethnoreligious ones, which have produced citizens who have had the moral and personal qualities to become leading contributors to society. African American churches, nonethnic churches, and many other religious groups have often played similar roles. Yet, although the value of such communities has often been recognized historically, and such communities have often been seen as contributing to the health of the nation, the mainstream culture has at the same time come to be defined in a way that would undermine such communities and minimize their public roles. That was certainly true of the 1950s, even though it was an era when the public consensus culture was reputed to be much more friendly to religious outlooks than it is today.

During the past two decades, there has been increasing recognition of the need to address the problem of religious pluralism in relation to the public domain. The message here, in the light of looking at some of the roots of the problem, is simply that such discussions need to continue, especially in the nation's shared intellectual life. It is true that when it comes to strongly held religious differences, there may be some insoluble problems. Some religious discourse allows no room for discussion with people of other outlooks. One irony in the present account is that, although it shows the long-term inadequacies of the American enlightenment's methods of dealing with religious difference, a pluralistic society still needs something like the enlightenment recognition that humans, despite their differences, share some beliefs in common. The enlightenment heritage, whatever its shortcomings, includes much that we all should value. A healthy society needs to be built on the basis of finding and cultivating those shared principles, even while honoring principled differences.

The most immediate practical application of what is here proposed would be that in public discussions there would not be prejudice against religiously based views simply because of their religious nature. People whose outlooks are shaped by religious perspectives might be expected to present their views through reasoned arguments that look for a common ground of widely shared concerns (such as the concern for equity in the present account). Yet there should be no assumption that outlooks reflecting trust in religious authority are second-class outlooks compared to those based on secular, naturalistic principles alone. Mid-twentieth-century outlooks still often assumed that there was a universal "objective reason" that self-evidently ought to trump viewpoints that involved religious authority. Secular viewpoints therefore became the gold standard for public discourse. That remained the case in the next generations, and the practice was reinforced by the ideal of the privatization of religion, as mainline Protestantism and expressions of civil religion receded. Yet there should be no prima facie assumption that purely naturalistic views are superior to religiously based views. Each sort of view, naturalistic or religious, should have equal opportunity to be heard and evaluated on its own merits by others in the public domain.

One place where such issues might be fruitfully addressed would be in mainstream academia. Ideally, the diverse academy should provide a model and a training ground for learning how people of various faiths, secular or religious, might work together in a public setting while taking their differences seriously. University administrators and academic departments might see one of their roles as being referees ensuring that all responsible voices, including explicitly religious voices, get a hearing on equitable terms appropriate to a public setting. To some extent that is already happening, and by many measures diverse religious outlooks seem to be taken more seriously in mainline academia than was true a quarter-century ago.[17]

Furthermore, in recent decades both Roman Catholic and evangelical intellectual communities have been providing valuable insights on these issues, and hence rich resources from which persons of other outlooks might learn. Just to speak of my own Protestant side, it is important to underscore that evangelicalism is far more complex than the present account of the populist religious right might suggest. The populist side of the movement thrives on polarizing dichotomies and for the past generation has cultivated polarized approaches to politics. But there has long been an evangelical left and also a wide variety of politically moderate evangelicals who do not fit the culture-wars stereotype. Among the most important evangelical resources that have been developing in recent years are its colleges, universities, and intellectual life. Due to its populist revivalist heritage, American evangelicalism often has been anti-intellectual or suspicious of any nuanced life of the mind. Yet, in the past generation, evangelicalism has been experiencing an intellectual renaissance notable especially for the cohort of excellent younger scholars. Evangelical colleges and universities have been thriving and have built outstanding faculties. These schools play important roles in strengthening evangelical subcommunities while preparing their graduates to participate in mainstream culture with understanding and with respect for views different from their own. Much of the thought at such schools is shaped, broadly speaking, by the Kuyperian tradition and its widely used motto, "the integration of faith and learning." One area where evangelical scholars in such schools and at other universities have been providing intellectual leadership has been in exploring how their particular religious faiths might be related to a genuine pluralism in the public sphere. Some of the best resources for addressing such issues may come from within the many-faceted evangelical community itself.[18]

Although my own outlook is shaped by Protestant Christian commitments, and this historical analysis has concentrated on the legacy of Protestantism as the most influential religious group shaping American culture, these proposals should apply to any religious subcommunity. One of the most significant changes that has taken place in the past half-century has been the vast increase in ethnic and religious diversity that has been fostered by new immigration policies. Accommodating religious diversity in American life today can no longer plausibly be talked about, as it was in the mid-twentieth century, in terms of "Protestant-Catholic-Jew." It is instead about equity for communities that represent virtually every religion in the world.

Finally, the sorts of people who are on center stage in this historical essay, public intellectuals, might play a leading role in facilitating discussions about the relation of the religious to the secular in the public domain. To some extent that, too, is already happening. The news media seem to now recognize the value of including different religious voices along with secular commentators, more so than they did a quarter-century ago. Furthermore, the Internet has provided public access to a huge variety of viewpoints. This access, though potentially helpful, can also be fragmenting, since most people go to sites that reinforce their preconceptions. What is needed is for the journalistic media, especially the outlets that still have access to a broad readership, to see one of their tasks as providing leadership in cultivating a public domain as fully inclusive of religiously shaped viewpoints as is feasible. Secularist commentators, rather than writing polemics denouncing religion in the name of universal reason, might better wrestle with the issues of how to respect both secular and religious viewpoints and institutions in the public domain. All sides need to recognize that we cannot go back to either a secular enlightenment or a Christian consensus, and that culture-war stances are not helpful alternatives. Rather, all sides need to recognize that they should be searching for ways to build a more fully inclusive pluralism.

Acknowledgments

THIS BOOK HAS BEEN GREATLY IMPROVED THROUGH the help of others. I am particularly grateful to my friends James Bratt, John Haas, Richard Mouw, William Svelmoe, Leonard Vander Zee, and Grant Wacker for reading all or parts of versions of this work and providing insightful comments. I am also thankful to be working once again with Lara Heimert, previously my principal editor for *Jonathan Edwards: A Life* (Yale University Press). She has been especially helpful in bringing this book into focus. Roger Labrie helped immensely in carrying through on the details of that enterprise. He combined impressive editorial skills with a fine knowledge of the historical era. The careful copyediting of Katherine Streckfus provided many improvements. Katy O'Donnell offered editorial assistance at various points in the process. Rachel King as project editor kept things running efficiently.

My greatest gratitude is, as always, to my wife, Lucie. I am all the more appreciative of her love and support during the years when this book was being written, a time when we each went through serious illness that helped us to reckon with our mortality and to appreciate the gifts of each day together.

Notes

Generally, the works by a single author pertaining to a given passage within a chapter are cited at the end of the passage, with page numbers appearing in the order cited.

INTRODUCTION

1. Alan Ehrenhalt, *The Lost City: The Forgotten Virtues of Community in America* (New York: Basic Books, 1995), 110, 265–267, 271.

2. Ross Douthat, *Bad Religion: How We Became a Nation of Heretics* (New York: Free Press, 2012); Tom Brokaw, *The Greatest Generation* (New York: Random House, 1998).

3. Arthur Miller's *Death of a Salesman* premiered in 1949 and was first published by Viking Press the same year. *Catcher in the Rye*, by J. D. Salinger, was published in 1951 by Little, Brown. The other quotations in this passage are references to David Riesman, *The Lonely Crowd* (New Haven, CT: Yale University Press, 1961 [1950]); Erich Fromm, *The Sane Society* (Greenwich, CT: Fawcett, 1965 [1955]); William Whyte, *The Organization Man* (Garden City, NY: Doubleday, 1957 [1956]); and Vance Packard, *The Status Seekers* (New York: Pocket Books, 1961 [1959]).

4. Ideally, analysis such as this should do more to place American thought in its European contexts and also involve more

comparative analysis. Those valuable features would make for a considerably longer and more technical book.

5. Lionel Trilling, *The Liberal Imagination: Essays on Literature and Society* (New York: Viking Press, 1950), ix. I also have avoided the "conservative" versus "liberal" debates of the time, largely because I am interested in the dominant moderate-liberal consensus outlook, and conservatism (aside from populist militant anticommunism) seemed much more a minority opinion then than it does today.

6. The debates among historians and philosophers about the meanings of "the enlightenment" are far too complex to enter into here. One simply has to recognize that the term can be used in many different ways and then define the way in which one is using it. Nonetheless, "the enlightenment" is still a useful shorthand for designating characteristic dominant patterns of eighteenth-century European thought, or, in the present case, eighteenth-century British-American thought, especially as manifested among the founders of the United States. Later postmodern critiques of "the enlightenment project" had roots at midcentury in the work of Max Horkheimer and Theodor Adorono, Jewish émigrés to the United States who published their seminal work in 1944 (in German). It was later translated into English as *Dialectic of Enlightenment* (New York: Herder and Herder, 1972).

7. Mark Noll, *America's God: From Jonathan Edwards to Abraham Lincoln* (New York: Oxford University Press, 2002), provides a valuable account of the merger of Protestant and enlightenment outlooks. Noll builds on Henry May's classic, *The Enlightenment in America* (New York: Oxford University Press, 1976), which provides an insightful account of the varieties of enlightenment thought.

8. At a late stage in working on this project, I am very pleased to see David A. Hollinger's "The Accommodation of Protestant Christianity with the Enlightenment: An Old Drama Still Being Enacted," in his *After Cloven Tongues of Fire: Protestant Liberalism*

in Modern American History (Princeton, NJ: Princeton University Press, 2013), 1–17, which puts emphasis parallel to my own on the interpretative importance of the enlightenment for understanding mid-twentieth-century culture and religion.

9. The best systematic exploration of the collapse of the Protestant establishment remains Robert Wuthnow, *The Restructuring of American Religion: Society and Faith Since World War II* (Princeton, NJ: Princeton University Press, 1988).

10. St. Augustine, or Augustine of Hippo, lived from 356 to 430. His theology is widely admired by many Roman Catholic, Eastern Orthodox, and Protestant (such as my own Reformed or Calvinistic) circles. To be Augustinian means to share in a classic orthodox heritage of basic Christian understandings and commitments. It also involves views on the relationship of faith and reason, as explained in the Conclusion.

Prologue: The National Purpose

1. The original series appeared in *Life* weekly from May 23 through June 20, 1960. The quotations in this section are from the book version, John K. Jessup, ed., *The National Purpose* (New York: Holt, Reinhart and Winston, 1960), as follows: Luce, v; Jessup, 17–18; Lippmann, 126–127, 130–131; Rossiter, 83; Gardner, 71–73; MacLeish, 37; Graham, 66–68, 62; Stevenson, 28; Wohlstetter, 95–102; Reston, 109. *Life*'s readership figure is stated in Daniel Bell, *The End of Ideology* (Glencoe, IL: Free Press, 1960), 34. The number is presumably based on the magazine typically being looked at by several family members. The magazine itself listed an "average circulation 6,700,000."

Chapter One: Mass Media and the National Character

1. David Halberstam, *The Fifties* (New York: Random House, 1993), 643–666, provides an engaging overview of this controversy to which I am much indebted.

2. John Steinbeck to Adlai Stevenson, November 5, 1959, *Steinbeck: A Life in Letters* (New York: Viking, 1975), 652; "Have We Gone Soft?" *The New Republic*, February 15, 1960, 11–15.

3. "Television History—The First 75 Years: 1959 NYC Evening Program Schedule," www.tvhistory.tv/1959-PrimeTime.jpg. Leonard Bernstein was also offering Young People's Concerts on Saturday afternoons.

4. Dwight Macdonald, "A Theory of Mass Culture," reprinted from *Diogenes* 1, no. 3 (1953): 1–17, in *Mass Culture: The Popular Arts in America*, Bernard Rosenberg and David Manning White, eds. (Glencoe, IL: Free Press, 1957), 59–73.

5. David Manning White, "Mass Culture in America: Another Point of View," an expanded version of "What's Happening to Mass Culture?" *Saturday Review* 39 (1956): 11–13, reprinted in *Mass Culture: The Popular Arts in America*, Bernard Rosenberg and David Manning White, eds. (Glencoe, IL: Free Press, 1957), 13–21.

6. Bernard Rosenberg, "Mass Culture in America," in *Mass Culture: The Popular Arts in America*, Bernard Rosenberg and David Manning White, eds. (Glencoe, IL: Free Press, 1957), 3–12.

7. Hannah Arendt, "Society and Culture," *Daedalus* 89, no. 2, Mass Culture and Mass Media Issue (1960): 284, 286.

8. James Baldwin, "Mass Culture and the Creative Artist: Some Personal Notes," *Daedalus* 89, no. 2, Mass Culture and Mass Media Issue (1960): 373–376.

9. Edwards Shils, "Mass Society and Its Culture," *Daedalus* 89, no. 2, Mass Culture and Mass Media Issue (1960): 290, 309, 314.

10. Norman Jacobs, "Introduction to the Issue on 'Mass Culture and Mass Media,'" *Daedalus* 89, no. 2, Mass Culture and Mass Media Issue (1960): 275.

11. The most famous symposium was "Our Country and Our Culture," *Partisan Review* 19, no. 3 (1952). For an overview of the discussions during the era, see Seymour Lipset, "Comments on 'American Intellectuals: Their Politics and Status,'" *Daedalus* 88, no. 3 (1959): 460–486. Other commentators on the topic in the

same issue included Arthur Schlesinger Jr., Karl Deutsch, Talcott Parsons, and Daniel Bell (pp. 487–498).

12. John Dewey, *A Common Faith* (New Haven, CT: Yale University Press, 1934).

13. Richard Hofstadter, *Anti-intellectualism in American Life* (New York: Vintage Books, 1963), 7, 117, 145, 159; Richard Hofstadter, *The Age of Reform* (New York: Vintage, 1955).

14. That was the argument of Russell Jacoby in *The Last Intellectuals: American Culture in the Age of Academe* (New York: Basic Books, 1987).

CHAPTER TWO: FREEDOM IN THE LONELY CROWD

1. Bernard Rosenberg, "Mass Culture in America," in *Mass Culture: The Popular Arts in America*, Bernard Rosenberg and David Manning White, eds. (Glencoe, IL: Free Press, 1957), 9.

2. Erich Fromm, *Escape from Freedom* (New York: Avon Books, 1965 [1941]. The list of Jewish émigrés is in Wilfred M. McClay, *The Masterless: Self and Society in Modern America* (Chapel Hill: University of North Carolina Press, 1994), 195–196. McClay's book also provides valuable analysis and background to many of the themes in this chapter.

3. Fromm, *Escape from Freedom*, viii, 208–209.

4. Ibid., 173, 186 (emphasis in original). Fromm's outlook was related to that of the heavy-duty intellectual theorists of the "Frankfurt School," Theodor Adorno, Max Horkheimer, and Herbert Marcuse. He shared their concern over "the authoritarian personality," as Adorno and his coauthors put it in their massive sociological and theoretical study (T. W. Adorno, Else Frenkel-Brunswik, Daniel J. Levinson, and R. Nevitt Sanford, *The Authoritarian Personality* [New York: Harper, 1950]). These philosophers decried "the enlightenment," but they themselves had great confidence in social scientific methods. Fromm had broken with these theorists over a number of issues. He also differed from them in that he could write engagingly in English.

5. Erich Fromm, *The Sane Society* (Greenwich, CT: Fawcett, 1965 [1955]), 309, 311, 64, cf. 17–19, 29–66, 122, 139–146, 315.

6. The brilliant intellectual historian Perry Miller had recently brought attention to the jeremiad as a favorite American Puritan genre. Miller himself celebrated Puritan intellectualism, joining others of his generation in lamenting America's decline to anti-intellectualism. See, especially, his two volumes on the subject, *The New England Mind: The Seventeenth Century* (Cambridge, MA: Harvard University Press, 1939), and *The New England Mind: From Colony to Province* (Cambridge, MA: Harvard University Press, 1953).

7. *The Sane Society* had gone through sixteen printings by 1966. Mainstream reviewers tended to be impressed by its insights, but they did point out that some of its psychological categories for interpreting history were speculative. See, for example, the review by Joseph Wood Krutch, *New York Times*, September 4, 1955, 9. Fromm's most popular book, *The Art of Loving* (1956) was a sort of how-to book. Learning how to love was an art, he suggested, and learning that art (and the alternatives to it) was the key to countering modern alienation.

James Hudnut-Beumler, in *Looking for God in the Suburbs: The Religion of the American Dream and Its Critics, 1945–1965* (New Brunswick, NJ: Rutgers University Press, 1994), 91, said that Riesman borrowed the concepts (although apparently not the exact phrases) "inner-directed" and "other-directed" from Fromm's *Man for Himself* (1947), and that Fromm adopted them from Martin Heidegger.

The commentator was Eric Larrabee, in "David Riesman and His Readers," in *Culture and Social Character: The Work of David Riesman Reviewed*, Seymour Martin Lipset and Leo Lowenthal, eds. (Glencoe, IL: Free Press, 1961), 406. The *Time* cover appeared on September 27, 1954, for the cover story entitled "Freedom—New Style."

8. This topic has been covered in many works. Martin Halliwell, *American Culture in the 1950s* (Edinburgh: University of

Edinburgh Press, 2007), provides a useful overview of culture at all levels. Another convenient introduction is David Castronovo, *Beyond the Gray Flannel Suit: Books from the 1950s That Made American Culture* (New York: Continuum, 2004).

9. David Riesman, *The Lonely Crowd* (New Haven, CT: Yale University Press, 1961 [1950]), xxxiii, 9–19, 19–24, 58–62, 37.

10. William Whyte, *The Organization Man* (Garden City, NY: Doubleday, 1957 [1956]), 11, 3, 7, 17, 31–32, 35, 13, 437, 443, 448.

11. Vance Packard, *The Hidden Persuaders* (New York: D. McKay, 1957), 200. Historian David Potter offered a more academic and judicious assessment of the role of advertising in his *People of Plenty: Economic Abundance and the American Character* (Chicago: University of Chicago Press, 1954). Potter put the subject in a historical framework, arguing that what had long made the United States distinctive was the presence of unprecedented abundance.

12. Vance Packard, *The Status Seekers* (New York: Pocket Books, 1961 [1959]), 316.

13. This example is taken from Daniel Bell, *The End of Ideology* (New York: Free Press, 1960), 35. Bell noted only that it was the December 1958 issue of *Reader's Digest*. The *Reader's Digest* circulation at the time was 12 million; *Women's Day*'s circulation was 5 million.

14. Betty Friedan, *The Feminine Mystique* (New York: W. W. Norton, 1997 [1963]). Ralph Ellison's novel *Invisible Man* (New York: Random House, 1952) was part of the discourse of the alienation of modern people as it related to African Americans. Though it was influential, it did not have the direct social impact of Friedan's work. In Friedan's book, as in other works on "modern man" in the era, African Americans remained invisible.

15. This summary of Friedan's early career draws on David Halberstam's account in *The Fifties* (New York: Random House, 1993), 592–598.

16. Friedan, *Feminine Mystique*, 425, 429, 434, 441, 450, 459–460.

17. The song "Me and Bobby Magee" was written by Kris Krist-offerson and Fred Foster and originally performed by Roger Miller in 1969.

CHAPTER THREE: ENLIGHTENMENT'S END? BUILDING WITHOUT FOUNDATIONS

1. John Dewey, *A Common Faith* (New Haven, CT: Yale University Press, 1934), 48.

2. Walter Lippmann, *Essays in the Public Philosophy* (Boston: Little, Brown, 1955).

3. Walter Lippmann, *Preface to Morals* (New York: Macmillan, 1929); Walter Lippmann, *The Cold War: A Study in U.S. Foreign Policy* (New York: Harper, 1947).

4. Lippmann, *Essays in the Public Philosophy*, 19–20, 100, 92, 156, 93–94.

5. Carl Binger, Lippmann's friend from childhood, used this phrase for his title in "A Child of the Enlightenment," in *Walter Lippmann and His Times*, Marquis Childs and James Reston, eds. (Freeport, NY: Books for Libraries Press, 1959), 21–36.

6. His classic summary of this idea is in William James, "What Pragmatism Means," Lecture II in a series of eight lectures on pragmatism that were published as *Pragmatism, a New Name for Some Old Ways of Thinking: Popular Lectures on Philosophy by William James* (New York: Longmans, Green, 1907). See also William James, *The Meaning of Truth: A Sequel to "Pragmatism"* (New York: Longmans, Green, 1909), and the exposition in James T. Kloppenberg, "Pragmatism: An Old Name for Some New Ways of Thinking?" *Journal of American History* 83, no. 1 (1996): 100–138. Kloppenberg contrasts James's realism to more radical pragmatists, such as Richard Rorty of the late twentieth century.

7. Quoted from Walter Lippmann, *A Preface to Politics* (Ann Arbor: University of Michigan Press, 1962 [1913]), 82–83, in John Patrick Diggins, *The Promise of Pragmatism: Modernism and the Crisis of Knowledge and Authority* (Chicago: University

of Chicago Press, 1994), 326; quoted from Walter Lippmann, *Drift and Mastery* (New York: Henry Holt, 1914), 285, in Arthur M. Schlesinger Jr., "Walter Lippmann: The Intellectual v. Politics," in *Walter Lippmann and His Times*, Marquis Childs and James Reston, eds. (Freeport, NY: Books for Libraries Press, 1959), 196.

8. Lippmann, *Preface to Morals*, 12, 144.

9. Joseph Wood Krutch, *The Modern Temper: A Study and a Confession* (New York: Harcourt, Brace, 1929); Carl L. Becker, *The Heavenly City of the Eighteenth Century Philosophers* (New Haven, CT: Yale University Press, 1932).

10. Ronald Steel, *Walter Lippmann and the American Century* (Boston: Little, Brown, 1980), 310–326, regarding Lippmann's views of the New Deal, as well as Lippmann's book on the subject, *The Good Society* (Boston: Little, Brown, 1937). Conservative reviews hailed his affirmation of a "higher law."

11. Paul Blanshard, *American Freedom and Catholic Power* (Boston: Beacon Press, 1949); William F. Buckley, *God and Man at Yale: The Superstitions of Academic Freedom* (Chicago: Regnery, 1951). Meanwhile, Father John Courtney Murray was in the process of rehabilitating the Catholic image in a series of scholarly presentations, which were eventually gathered into his influential *We Hold These Truths: Catholic Reflections on the American Proposition* (New York: Sheed and Ward, 1960). In these presentations he argued that the natural-law ideals of the founders had continuities with the ideas of Thomas Aquinas and Catholicism.

12. During the late 1930s, Lippmann had been temporarily attracted to Catholicism; see Steel, *Walter Lippmann and the American Century*, 491–492. Edward A. Purcell Jr., in *The Crisis of Democratic Theory: Scientific Naturalism and the Problem of Value* (Lexington: University Press of Kentucky, 1973), 154, noted that, at least when Lippmann first started talking about natural law in the late 1930s, his concept of natural law was not even metaphysical but was based on a historical and cultural process of rational

deductions from immutable principles. Lippmann was not alone among prominent non-Catholic thinkers in advocating natural law; Robert Hutchins, former president of the University of Chicago, and Hutchins's friend and associate Mortimer Adler were the best known. See Steel, *Walter Lippmann and the American Century*, 494–495, for a summary of the reviews.

13. Archibald MacLeish, "The Alternative," *Yale Review* 44, no. 4 (1955): 492, 495.

14. Walter Lippmann, "A Rejoinder," *Yale Review* 44, no. 4 (1955): 499–500 (emphasis in original).

15. Schlesinger, "Walter Lippmann: The Intellectual v. Politics," 219–222.

16. Arthur Schlesinger Jr., *The Vital Center: The Politics of Freedom* (New York: Houghton Mifflin, 1949), 254, 156, 256.

17. Daniel Bell, *The End of Ideology: On the Exhaustion of Political Ideas in the Fifties* (Glencoe, IL: Free Press, 1960), 22–36, 372–374. Nathan Liebowitz, in *Daniel Bell and the Agony of Modern Liberalism* (Westport, CT: Greenwood Press, 1985), 9–39, puts Bell's views into context and associates them with those of Seymour Lipset, Edward Shils, and Raymond Aron.

18. Arthur M. Schlesinger Jr., "Sources of the New Deal," in *Paths to American Thought*, Arthur M. Schlesinger Jr. and Morton White, eds. (New York: Houghton Mifflin, 1963), 389; Daniel Bell, "Introduction," in *The New American Right*, Daniel Bell, ed. (New York: Criterion Books, 1955), 4, 17, 27. The essay was also in Bell, *End of Ideology*. Daniel J. Boorstin developed a very similar reading of American history in *The Genius of American Politics* (Chicago: University of Chicago Press, 1953). Boorstin wrote, for instance, "A pretty good rule of thumb for us in the United States is that our national well-being is in inverse proportion to the sharpness and extent of theoretical differences between our political parties" (p. 3).

19. Robert Booth Fowler, *Believing Skeptics: America Political Intellectuals, 1945–1964* (Westport, CT: Greenwood Press, 1978).

Purcell, *Crisis in Democratic Theory*, offers a particularly trenchant analysis of this dominant outlook, which he designates as "relativist democratic theory." See also Richard H. Pells, *The Liberal Mind in a Conservative Age* (New York: Harper and Row, 1985).

20. Robert Dahl, *A Preface to Democratic Theory* (Chicago: University of Chicago Press, 1956), 45, 151; Louis Hartz, quoted from "Democracy: Image and Reality," in *Democracy in the Mid-20th Century*, W. N. Chambers and R. N. Salisbury, eds. (St. Louis: Washington University, 1960), 29, in Purcell, *Crisis of Democratic Theory*, 258.

21. Schlesinger, *Vital Center*, 190, 191.

22. Edward Purcell observed that "civil liberties and civil rights could well have helped reform-minded intellectuals overlook the fundamental status quo orientation of their theory." Purcell, *Crisis of Democratic Theory*, 255.

23. This paragraph and the next are dependent on David Chappell, *A Stone of Hope: Prophetic Religion and the Death of Jim Crow* (Chapel Hill: University of North Carolina Press, 2004), 27–28, 207n, quoting Schlesinger, *Vital Center*, 20, 190. Chappell sees the influential book *An American Dilemma: The Negro Problem and American Democracy*, by Gunnar Myrdal, with the assistance of Richard Sterner and Arnold Rose (New York: Harper Brothers, 1944), as among the leading instances of faith in the progressive acceptance of the "American creed," promoted through education, as the best hope for resolving race (p. 42).

24. See, for example, Taylor Branch, *Parting the Waters: America in the King Years, 1954–63* (New York: Simon and Schuster, 1988).

25. On personalism, see the quotation from Martin Luther King Jr., *Stride Toward Freedom* (New York: Perennial Library, 1964 [1958]), 82, quoted in Ira G. Zepp Jr., *The Social Vision of Martin Luther King, Jr.* (Brooklyn, NY: Carlson, 1989), 173; for God placing moral laws within the structure of the universe, see Martin Luther King Jr., *Strength to Love* (New York: Harper and Row, 1963), 128, quoted in Zepp, *Social Vision*, 198. Zepp offers a

careful survey of these philosophical and theological views. He observes, "Whatever else King firmly believed, he affirmed the moral structure of the universe" (p. 198).

26. King, *Strength to Love*, 115, and other quotations, quoted in Zepp, *Social Vision*, 196, 211.

27. Martin Luther King Jr., *I Have a Dream: Writings and Speeches That Changed the World*, James Melvin Washington, ed. (San Francisco: HarperSanFrancisco, 1986), 89.

CHAPTER FOUR: THE PROBLEM OF AUTHORITY: THE TWO MASTERS

1. William Barrett, *Irrational Man: A Study in Existential Philosophy* (Garden City, NY: Doubleday, 1962 [1958]), 34, 36, 275, 269, 276, 279, 271, 4–7.

2. I am indebted to Richard Lints's helpful account of "foundationalism" in *Progressive and Conservative Religious Ideologies: The Tumultuous Decade of the 1960s* (Burlington, VT: Ashgate, 2010), 145–149.

3. A. J. Ayer, *Language, Truth and Logic* (New York: Dover, 1952 [1946]), 46, 119, 107–108.

4. See, for instance, Nicholas Wolterstorff, "Scholarship Grounded in Religion," in *Religion, Scholarship, and Higher Education: Perspectives, Models and Future Prospects*, Andrea Sterk, ed. (Notre Dame, IN: University of Notre Dame Press, 2002), 3–15. Cf. Lints, *Progressive and Conservative Religious Ideologies*.

5. B. F. Skinner, "Baby in a Box," *Ladies' Home Journal*, October 1945.

6. B. F. Skinner, *Walden Two* (New York: Macmillan, 1948); Aldous Huxley, *Brave New World* (New York: Harper and Brothers, 1932); B. F. Skinner, *Science and Human Behavior* (New York: Macmillan, 1953), 427.

7. Skinner, *Science and Human Behavior*, 5, 7, 9, 5, 20, 439.

8. Various other earlier figures, such as Karen Horney and Harry Stack Sullivan, whom Rogers acknowledged as predeces-

sors, provided theories of personality that were more positive than Freud's. Rogers's post-Freudian optimism also has similarities to Erich Fromm's. Jason W. Stevens, *God-Fearing and Free: A Spiritual History of America's Cold War* (Cambridge, MA: Harvard University Press, 2010), 185–219, provides a detailed account of these developments.

9. Carl Rogers, *Client-Centered Therapy: Its Current Practice, Implications, and Theory* (Boston: Houghton Mifflin, 1951), 4, 6.

10. "Some Issues Concerning the Control of Human Behavior: A Symposium, Carl R. Rogers and B. F. Skinner," *Science* 124 (1956): 1057–1065; republished in Richard I. Evans, *Carl Rogers: The Man and His Ideas* (New York: E. P. Dutton, 1965), xliv–lxxxviii.

11. Margaret Mead, *Coming of Age in Samoa: A Psychological Study of Primitive Youth for Western Civilization* (New York: Blue Ribbon Books, 1928); Ruth Benedict, *Patterns of Culture* (Boston: Houghton Mifflin, 1934); Alfred C. Kinsey, Wardell B. Pomeroy, and Clyde E. Martin, *Sexual Behavior in the Human Male* (Philadelphia: W. B. Saunders, 1948); Alfred C. Kinsey, Wardell B. Pomeroy, Clyde E. Martin, and Paul H. Gebhard, *Sexual Behavior in the Human Female* (Philadelphia, W. B. Saunders, 1953).

12. The idea that the 1960s accelerated trends already under way is the argument of Alan Petigny in *The Permissive Society: America, 1941–1965* (New York: Cambridge University Press, 2009). Other works cited here are Grace Metalious, *Peyton Place* (New York: Messner, 1956); Vladimir Nabokov, *Lolita* (New York: G. P. Putnam's Sons, 1958); D. H. Lawrence, *Lady Chatterley's Lover* (New York: Grove Press, 1959).

13. Benjamin Spock, *The Common Sense Book of Baby and Child Care* (New York: Pocket Books, 1946); Thomas Maier, *Dr. Spock: An American Life* (New York: Harcourt, Brace, 1998), 200.

14. The quotations are from the first edition, page numbers not given, in Maier, *Dr. Spock*, 129, 136. Cf. Petigny, *Permissive Society*, 39–40, 227 (emphasis in original).

15. Christopher Lasch, *The Culture of Narcissism* (New York: Warner, 1979, 22, 114, 116, 119, 103.

16. Robert N. Bellah, Richard Madsen, William M. Sullivan, Ann Swidler, and Steven M. Tipton, *Habits of the Heart: Individualism and Commitment in American Life* (Berkeley: University of California Press, 1985), 47. For an insightful and more recent take on aspects of these trends, see David Brooks, *Bobos in Paradise: The New Upper Class and How They Got There* (New York: Simon and Schuster, 2000). Brooks relates his analysis specifically to the social critiques of the 1950s.

CHAPTER FIVE: THE LATTER DAYS OF THE PROTESTANT ESTABLISHMENT

1. Robert D. Putnam and David E. Campbell, *American Grace: How Religion Divides and Unites Us* (New York: Simon and Schuster, 2010), 87, citing George Gallup and D. Michael Lindsay, *Surveying the Religious Landscape: Trends in US. Beliefs* (Harrisburg, PA: Morehouse, 1999), 7, 19; Sidney E. Ahlstrom, *A Religious History of the American People* (New Haven, CT: Yale University Press, 1972), 952.

2. John K. Jessup, ed., *The Ideas of Henry Luce* (New York: Atheneum, 1969), 282. Luce sometimes did make a distinction, but he also often lapsed into conflation, as in "God of Our Fathers," a centennial speech at Lake Forest College in which he spoke of the specifically Presbyterian heritage, but ended by saying, "We Americans, in relation to the future, stand about where Joshua stood," essentially equating America's mission with that of ancient Israel. Jessup, ed., *Ideas of Henry Luce*, 324.

3. David Sarnoff, "The Fabulous Future," and John von Neumann, "Can We Survive Technology?" in *The Fabulous Future: America in 1980*, by the Editors of Fortune (New York: E. P. Dutton, 1956), 18, 37. In Sarnoff's view, moreover, "the interdependence of people in a world shrunk by science inevitably requires broader mental concepts, which would lead to great ethical and moral stature—which in turn stimulate man's spiritual growth" (p. 26).

4. Henry R. Luce, "A Speculation About 1980," in *The Fabulous Future: America in 1980*, by the Editors of Fortune (New York: E. P. Dutton, 1956), 183–184; "the public philosophy" quotation is from a speech at St. Louis University, November 16, 1955, quoted in Jessup, ed., *Ideas of Henry Luce*, 166–167.

5. Luce, "A Speculation About 1980," 195, 198–199 (emphasis in original). Luce later discovered Pierre Teilhard de Chardin, who also enunciated ideas about the evolving collaboration between people and God; Luce even used the pages of *Life* in 1964 to promote the complex views of the scientist-theologian to the general public. See Jessup, ed., *Ideas of Henry Luce*, 324–335.

6. Jacques Ellul, *The Technological Society* (New York: Knopf, 1964), xxv.

7. Paul Blanshard, *American Freedom and Catholic Power* (Boston: Beacon Press, 1949); John Courtney Murray, *We Hold These Truths: Catholic Reflections on the American Proposition* (New York: Sheed and Ward, 1960).

8. See William Inboden, *Religion and American Foreign Policy: The Soul of Containment* (Cambridge, UK: Cambridge University Press, 2008); Jason W. Stevens, *God-Fearing and Free: A Spiritual History of America's Cold War* (Cambridge, MA: Harvard University Press, 2010).

9. Martin Marty, *The New Shape of American Religion* (New York: Harper and Row, 1959), 39, 74.

10. Will Herberg, *Protestant-Catholic-Jew* (New York: Doubleday, 1955).

11. Blake is quoted in Marty, *New Shape*, 77.

12. Marty, *New Shape*, 10, 31–44, 77, 79, 83, 110.

13. Morton White, "Original Sin, Natural Law, and Politics" (1956), in *Religion, Politics, and the Higher Learning: A Collection of Essays* (Cambridge, MA: Harvard University Press, 1959), 117–118.

14. Reinhold Niebuhr, *The Irony of American History* (New York: Scribner's, 1952), 138.

15. Andrew S. Finstuen, *Original Sin and Everyday Protestants: The Theology of Reinhold Niebuhr* (Chapel Hill: University of North Carolina Press, 2009); White, "Original Sin, 117–118. Finstuen makes the point that the doctrine of original sin enjoyed considerable popularity.

16. Niebuhr, *Irony*, 110, 7, 1–16.

17. Ibid., 80. Niebuhr also quoted psychologist Gordon Allport as using a similar analogy (p. 81n). Cf. Reinhold Niebuhr, *Moral Man and Immoral Society* (New York: Scribner's, 1932), xiii, where he quotes Dewey. In discussing Niebuhr's critique of Dewey in *Professor Reinhold Niebuhr: A Mentor to the Twentieth Century* (Louisville, KY: Westminster/John Knox, 1992), Ronald H. Stone cites Dewey as recognizing, by 1936 at least, that the obstacles to creating a scientifically based society could be insuperable (p. 230; cf. 210–214).

18. Reinhold Niebuhr, "Ideology and the Scientific Method" (1953), in *The Essential Reinhold Niebuhr*, Robert McAfee Brown, ed. (New Haven, CT: Yale University Press, 1986), 210, 215.

19. Reinhold Niebuhr, *Christian Realism and Political Problems* (New York: Scribner's, 1953), 175, quoted in Ronald H. Stone, *Professor Reinhold Niebuhr: A Mentor to the Twentieth Century* (Louisville, KY: Westminster/John Knox, 1992), 207–208. On Niebuhr's relationship to pragmatism and to James and Dewey, see Stone, *Professor Reinhold Niebuhr*, 205–215, and Martin Halliwell, *The Constant Dialogue: Reinhold Niebuhr and American Intellectual Culture* (Lanham, MD: Rowman and Littlefield, 2005), 19–78.

20. Reinhold Niebuhr, "Coherence, Incoherence, and Christian Faith" (1951), in *The Essential Reinhold Niebuhr*, Robert McAfee Brown, ed. (New Haven, CT: Yale University Press, 1986), 232–233. As usual, Niebuhr saw his view regarding faith and reason as standing between two extremes: Roman Catholic neo-Thomism, which put too much trust in reason, and the radical neo-orthodoxy of Karl Barth, which put no trust at all in natural human wisdom or natural theology. Ibid., 226–231.

21. Morton White himself made this point in offering a scathing attack on Protestant attempts to retain their privilege in higher education. All of these attempts, he said, tried "to avoid identifying religion with any claim to knowledge that might have to run the gauntlet of scientific test." Morton White, "Religion, Politics, and the Higher Learning" (1954), in *Religion, Politics, and the Higher Learning* (Cambridge, MA: Harvard University Press, 1959), 89.

22. Reinhold Niebuhr, "Pious and Secular America" (1957), in *Pious and Secular America* (New York: Scribner's, 1958), 1, 2, 4, 13.

23. David A. Hollinger provides some insightful reflections on this point in "Epilogue: Reinhold Niebuhr and Protestant Liberalism," in *After Cloven Tongues of Fire: Protestant Liberalism in Modern American History* (Princeton, NJ: Princeton University Press, 2013), 211–225.

24. The term is borrowed from Peter L. Berger, *The Sacred Canopy: Elements of a Sociological Theory of Religion* (Garden City, NY: Doubleday, 1967).

CHAPTER SIX: SEQUEL: CONSENSUS BECOMES A FIGHTING WORD

1. The terminology can sometimes be confusing. Much of the conservative side of American Protestantism has been shaped by the revivalist tradition. Emphasizing the authority of the Bible, and the necessity of personal conversion made possible by the redemptive work of Christ on the cross, this revivalist tradition was also known as "evangelical." In the early twentieth century, in reaction to modernism in theology and changes in cultural mores, many of these evangelical revivalists were involved in the "fundamentalist" movement, which was characterized by particularly militant opposition to those trends. By the 1950s, some of the heirs to fundamentalism were adopting a somewhat more moderate tone and calling themselves "neo-evangelical" or just "evangelical." Billy Graham, who began his career as a fundamentalist, became associated with this new evangelicalism. The revivalist heritage, or evangelicalism, includes many separate denominations and

submovements, so it is sometimes necessary to use a variety of these terms to cover all who are involved. For a more complete analysis, see George Marsden, *Fundamentalism and American Culture*, 2nd ed. (New York: Oxford University Press, 2005 [1980]), and especially the chart regarding terminology, 234–235.

2. For examples, see the bibliographies offered at the website of the Institute for the Study of American Evangelicals at www .wheaton.edu/isae.

3. Tim LaHaye, *The Spirit-Controlled Temperament* (Wheaton, IL: Tyndale House, 1966); James C. Dobson, *Dare to Discipline* (Wheaton, IL: Tyndale House, 1970). Randall J. Stephen and Karl W. Giberson, *The Anointed: Evangelical Truth in a Secular Age* (Cambridge, MA: Belknap Press of Harvard University Press, 2011), 97–138, provides a helpful introduction, on which I am drawing here. On the background of evangelical alternative psychologies I am indebted to Daniel DuBois Gottwig, "Before the Culture Wars: Conservative Protestants and the Family, 1920–1980," PhD dissertation, University of Notre Dame, 2011.

4. Alan Ehrenhalt points this out in *The Lost City: The Forgotten Virtues of Community in America* (New York: Basic Books, 1995), 21. Ehrenhalt also explains that in fact the sense of community was more widespread in America in the 1950s than it was in later decades.

5. For a biography of Francis Schaeffer, see Barry Hankins, *Francis Schaeffer and the Shaping of Evangelical America* (Grand Rapids, MI: Wm. B. Eerdmans, 2008). For more information about Francis Schaeffer's son Frank, see Frank Schaeffer, *Crazy for God: How I Grew Up as One of the Elect, Helped Found the Religious Right, and Lived to Take All (or Almost All) of It Back* (New York: Carroll and Graf, 2007); on the making of the films, I drew from p. 266 of this work. The book versions were Francis A. Schaeffer, *How Should We Then Live? The Rise and Decline of Western Thought and Culture* (Old Tappan, NJ: Revell, 1976), and Francis A. Schaeffer and C. Everett Koop, *Whatever Happened to the*

Human Race? Exposing Our Rapid Yet Subtle Loss of Human Rights (Old Tappan, NJ: Revell, 1979).

6. Francis A. Schaeffer, *How Should We Then Live?* (1976), in *The Complete Works of Francis A. Schaeffer*, vol. 5, 2nd ed. (Wheaton, IL: Crossway, 1985), 226. Schaeffer had just cited both Daniel Bell and economist John Kenneth Galbraith on the increasing role of elites in modern technological society (pp. 223–224). Tim LaHaye, *The Battle for the Mind: A Subtle Warfare* (Old Tappan, NJ: Revell, 1980).

7. Falwell is quoted in Ronald A. Wells, "Schaeffer in America," in Ronald W. Ruegsegger, ed., *Reflections on Francis Schaeffer* (Grand Rapids, MI: Zondervan, 1980), 234. The quotations by Schaeffer are in Francis A. Schaeffer, *A Christian Manifesto* (Wheaton, IL: Crossway, 1981), 424, 482. Schaeffer often used the term "humanism" to refer to "secular humanism," a human-centered philosophy based on the belief in an impersonal, chance universe.

8. Francis A. Schaeffer, *The Great Evangelical Disaster* (1984), in *The Complete Works of Francis A. Schaeffer*, vol. 4, 2nd ed. (Wheaton, IL: Crossway, 1985), 416n. Schaeffer said there was never a "golden age" and allowed that there had been flaws at the time of consensus, including racism and earlier slavery, the wrong use of wealth, and identification of America as God's "chosen nation" (pp. 416–417). Darren Dochuk, in *From Bible Belt to Sunbelt: Plainfolk Religion, Grassroots Politics, and the Rise of Evangelical Conservatism* (New York: W. W. Norton, 2011), provides an insightful account of the sense of longing for more Christian-friendly times and places during this era, especially among those who had migrated to Southern California. The mid-1930s was when, according to Schaeffer, his former denomination, the mainline northern Presbyterian Church (U.S.A.), had become apostate, so that he believed it necessary to separate from that prestigious institution. He was part of the fundamentalist Bible Presbyterian Church, led by Carl McIntire, from 1937 to 1956. Thus Schaeffer usually dated the American turning point as in the 1930s.

9. Francis A. Schaeffer, "Special Note to Christians," in *How Should We Then Live?* (1976), in *The Complete Works of Francis A. Schaeffer*, vol. 5, 2nd ed. (Wheaton, IL: Crossway, 1985), 255 (emphasis in original).

10. Francis A. Schaeffer, "Foreword," in John W. Whitehead, *The Second American Revolution* (Elgin, IL: David C. Cook, 1982).

11. Quite a few authors have suggested that the religious right is more pervasively shaped by a movement, often called "Reconstructionism," dedicated to reinstituting "theonomy," or Old Testament law. For example, see Kevin Phillips, *American Theocracy* (New York: Viking, 2006). Sometimes Francis Schaeffer is represented as promoting such views because he borrowed some historical analysis from Reconstructionist founder Rousas J. Rushdoony. However, according to Frank Schaeffer, *Sex, Mom, and God* (Cambridge, MA: DaCapo Press, 2011), 110, Francis Schaeffer often referred to Rushdoony's full-blown Reconstructionist scheme as "insanity." See also Hankins, *Francis Schaeffer and the Shaping of Evangelical America*, 193–194. Accusations that Reconstructionism is widespread in the movement fail to take into account the extent to which most conservative evangelicals are committed to the American political heritage.

12. David Barton, *The Jefferson Lies: Exposing the Myths You've Always Believed About Thomas Jefferson* (Nashville: Thomas Nelson, 2012). The book's many inaccuracies were exposed by Warren Throckmorton and Michael Coulter in *Getting Jefferson Right: Fact Checking Claims About Our Third President* (Grove City, PA: Salem Grove Press, 2012).

13. I am not saying, of course, that no one in the Protestant religious right addressed such issues, only that the popular calls for a return to a "Christian America" contributed to a characteristic neglect of that issue. See Conclusion, note 8.

CONCLUSION: TOWARD A MORE INCLUSIVE PLURALISM

1. Arthur M. Schlesinger Jr., "Walter Lippmann: The Intellectual v. Politics," in *Walter Lippmann and His Times,* Marquis Childs

and James Reston, eds. (Freeport, NY: Books for Libraries Press, 1959), 222; David Riesman, *The Lonely Crowd* (New Haven, CT: Yale University Press, 1961 [1950]), 37.

2. The term "the noble dream" is from Peter Novick, *That Noble Dream: The "Objectivity Question" and the American Historical Profession* (Cambridge, UK: Cambridge University Press, 1988).

3. Thomas S. Kuhn, *The Structure of Scientific Revolutions* (Chicago: University of Chicago Press, 1962).

4. C. S. Lewis, *Surprised by Joy: the Shape of My Early Life* (New York: Harcourt, Brace, 1995 [1955]), 201.

5. I provide much fuller argumentation for these views regarding higher education in my book *The Outrageous Idea of Christian Scholarship* (New York: Oxford University Press, 1997).

6. For mainstream America's failure to address religious diversity, see David Sehat, *The Myth of American Religious Freedom* (New York: Oxford University Press, 2011), which provides a valuable overview and interpretation of these issues.

7. A good indication of their inattention to religion is found in Daniel Roger's *The Age of Fracture* (Cambridge, MA: Harvard University Press, 2011). The subject of how to deal with religious diversity arose only indirectly in this impressively comprehensive recounting of mainstream intellectual trends of the late twentieth century.

8. Since the 1980s, a good bit of the recent thought on the topic of religious and cultural diversity has come from Roman Catholic thinkers. Philosopher Alasdair MacIntyre, for instance, offers important perspectives on intellectual pluralism in *Three Rival Versions of Moral Inquiry* (Notre Dame, IN: University of Notre Dame Press, 1990). Richard John Neuhaus, a convert from Lutheranism in 1990, wrote much on the topic, most famously, *The Naked Public Square: Religion and Democracy in America* (Grand Rapids, MI: Wm. B. Eerdmans, 1986). He also provided a neoconservative forum for discussing such subjects in his intellectual journal, *First Things*, founded in 1990.

Protestant conservatives as well as Catholics have made recent contributions to the discussion. A nice sampling is found in Hugh Heclo and Wilfred M. McClay, eds., *Religion Returns to the Public Square: Faith and Policy in America* (Baltimore: Johns Hopkins University Press, 2003). The necessities of practical politics have also forced attention to the issue. E. J. Dionne Jr. remarks in the Foreword to that work that the goal expressed by political strategist Ralph Reed, of simply asking for "a place at the table," "represents a true triumph of religious pluralism" (p. xiv).

For an account of how nuanced views of Christians on such topics are eclipsed by simplistic populist views, see Randall J. Stephens and Karl W. Giberson, *The Anointed: Evangelical Truth in a Secular Age* (Cambridge, MA: Harvard University Press, 2011).

9. For understanding Kuyper in his own time, see the excellent biography by James D. Bratt, *Abraham Kuyper: Modern Calvinist, Christian Democrat* (Grand Rapids, MI: Wm. B. Eerdmans, 2013).

10. Abraham Kuyper, *Principles of Sacred Theology*, trans. J. Hendrik De Vries (Grand Rapids, MI: Baker Book House, 1980 [1898]), 150–159.

11. Ibid. Cf. "Common Grace in Science" (1901), in *Abraham Kuyper: A Centennial Reader*, James D. Bratt, ed. (Grand Rapids, MI: Wm. B. Eerdmans, 1998), 441–460.

12. Kuyper, *Principles of Sacred Theology*.

13. For another introduction to the views I am endorsing here, see James W. Skillen, *Recharging the American Experiment: Principled Pluralism for Genuine Civil Community* (Grand Rapids, MI: Baker Books, 1994). For a briefer summary, see Corwin Smidt, "The Principled Pluralist Perspective," in *Church, State and Public Justice: Five Views*, P. C. Kemeny, ed. (Downers Grove, IL: IVP Academic, 2007), 127–153. The Center for Public Justice website provides an extensive bibliography on the subject at www.cpjustice.org/content/christianity-politics-bibliography. Regarding the Court's recommendations for objective study of religion in *Abington Township v. Schempp* (1963), see Warren A. Nord's dis-

cussion of such opinions and of the problem of the biases of such "neutrality" in *Religion and American Education: Rethinking a National Dilemma* (Chapel Hill: University of North Carolina Press, 1995), 236–261.

14. For the background of the epistemological differences between the American conservative Protestant commonsense heritage and Kuyper's outlook, see "The Evangelical Love Affair with Enlightenment Science" in George Marsden, *Understanding Fundamentalism and Evangelicalism* (Grand Rapids, MI: Wm. B. Eerdmans, 1991), 122–152. The creation science movement is the best example of conservative Protestant claims that objective scientific study will support traditional interpretations of the Bible.

15. On "mediating institutions," cf. Richard J. Mouw, *Abraham Kuyper: A Short and Personal Introduction* (Grand Rapids, MI: Wm. B. Eerdmans, 2011), 42–44.

16. For example, Douglas Jacobsen and Rhonda Jacobsen, eds., *The American University in a Postsecular Age* (New York: Oxford University Press, 2008).

17. See, for instance, John Schmalzbauer and Kathleen Mahoney, "Religion and Knowledge in the Post-Secular Academy," in *The Post-Secular in Question: Religion in Contemporary Society*, Philip S. Gorski, David Kyuman Kim, and Jonathan Van Antwerpen, eds. (New York: New York University Press, 2012), 215–248.

18. See David Swartz, *Moral Minority: The Evangelical Left in and Age of Conservatism* (Philadelphia: University of Pennsylvania Press, 2012). For a nice sampling of the variety of views that have been shaping evangelical outlooks, see P. C. Kemeny, ed., *Church, State and Public Justice: Five Views* (Downers Grove, IL: IVP Academic, 2007).

Index